An exceptional resource for accelerating healing, combining the power of compassion with the science of mantras, visualization and meditation.

—Dannion Brinkley, New York Times bestselling author "Saved by the Light" and "Secrets of the Light" with Kathryn Brinkley

I never experienced until now how words and even sounds could change me so much. When I get into my heart and do these mantras, it's thrilling! Josefine brings Kuan Yin's timeless tools for higher consciousness up-to-date with the latest science of Heartsound.

—Denis Ouellette, author "Heal Yourself with Breath, Light, Sound & Water," publisher of NaturalLifeNews.com

Without question, Kuan Yin is key to the transformation that is now happening for us personally and globally. Her love and mercy will heal us, even while her vision for us will catapult us into a brighter, freer future. But for her to be able to do what she can for us, we need to open our hearts and invite her in. We must get to know this beautiful goddess. Josefine shows us how and provides us with numerous tools to call Kuan Yin into our lives.

—Dawn Covington, Ed.D., President & Founder of NewWisdom University, co-author "Healing Our Planet, Healing Our Selves"

When you need a solution and want to pray but don't know where to begin, Kuan Yin's Miracle Mantras will guide you to the place of peace within your heart. This book is a true companion for anyone walking a spiritual path.

—Alberta Fredricksen, author "Awaken Your Inner Peacemaker" and "Resume of a Disciple: Stepping Up Spiritually"

In Eastern traditions, Kuan Yin has long been the keeper of unconditional love and compassion — the frequencies of the spiritual heart. Josefine Stark has written a beautiful and comprehensive book about this divine being. Her book is full of history, legend and stories about Kuan Yin, but more importantly, it contains many exercises and practices that can help you to connect with her and to open your heart. In today's world of violence, anger, sorrow and pain, this book is sorely needed.

—*Shaeri Richards, author "Dancing with your Dragon: The Art of Loving your Unlovable Self"*

This book on Kuan Yin is a masterpiece, a miracle and a mantra all in one—a well-rounded integration of her history, teachings, mantras and sutras. It also covers accelerating on the spiritual path through the use of compassion, the powers of sound, and the violet light. I enjoyed reading about her lifetimes and miracle stories.

—*William Star, B.A. in Psychology, creator of AnOpenDoorOfLove.org*

A power-packed book with abundant information of real spiritual magnetism! From learning to open and use the heart for extending compassion and forgiveness, to developing visualization, to dissolving negative karma, this book not only provides solid, research-based science, but also detailed practical how-to's for applying the principles. It including detailed use of mantras, mudras, the fabulous Sutras, the violet fire, crystals and more! Best of all, it leads one on a path of devotion to God via the compassionate manifestation of the Divine Feminine—Kuan Yin!

—*James Berwick, LCSW, psychotherapist*

The power of mantra is profound. Not only do the heart, breath, and mind engage in a symphonic dance, but also the vibrations created create profound changes that enable shifts in the energy of the biofield for healing. Employing the mantras in this book will produce great benefit!

—*Alexandra Soteriou, MA in Health & Healing, author "Gift of the Conquerors: Hand Paper-Making in India"*

This book brings new and well-written insights into the study of Kuan Yin. It is crammed with carefully researched and fascinating lore unavailable from any other single source. Clearly, it comes straight from the heart.

—J.Douglas Kenyon, editor "Atlantis Rising Magazine,"
author "Forbidden Religion: Suppressed Heresies of the West"

Inspiring and enlightening! Josefine brings Kuan Yin into the Age of Aquarius with this intelligently written, practical and accessible offering for both beginning students and advanced devotees who are walking the Bodhisattva Path. Highly recommended!

— David Milak, owner Sacred Mysteries Bookstore

As a lover of legends and true stories of the miraculous, I found this a fascinating book about a great spiritual being little known outside of Asia. I learned of Kuan Yin's healings and intercession, both ancient and modern, which will inspire the reader to take up her powerful mantras. I've enjoyed listening to Buddhist children reciting them, but didn't know the words or their meanings until finding them here. With chapters on the miraculous Heart Sutras and others on mudras (hand gestures) and crystals, this book is a treasure trove for anyone who desires to explore the realms of the Goddess of Mercy.

—Wayne H. Purdin, author "The SOLution: Laying the Foundation for a Solar
Civilization" and "Lessons on the Path" and editor of "Sun Gazette" at
SunCenterOfPhoenix.com

A remarkable blend of ancient wisdom and quantum science that includes practical methods to access the power of the heart through sound, mantra, and visualization in order to help evolve our souls and transform the planet.

—Ronnie Foster, ordained minister, intuitive counselor, hospice volunteer and
national trainer for "The Twilight Brigade" and "Compassion in Action"

A must-read for anyone serious about understanding the ancient wisdom of the Chinese mantras (with the aid of translations and pronunciation guides) and their practical use for us today. An excellent job of researching and synthesizing Kuan Yin's teachings with a modern understanding of energy and power, from ancient mantras, to the science of sound, to an understanding of quantum physics. I recommend this book for all who want a practical guide in applying eternal truths for healing and expanding the powers of the heart.

—*Rev.Carl Showalter, MTh, founder and director of "Quantum Living Institute" and the worldwide movement,"Spiritual Awareness Fellowship"*

The most comprehensive book on Kuan Yin to my knowledge! Extensively researched and full of interesting information, along with simple yet powerful mantras and meditation practices that will transform your life.

—*Dr. Jin K. Robertson, author "Major Dream: From Immigrant Housemaid to Harvard Ph.D."*

KUAN YIN'S MIRACLE MANTRAS

*Awakening
the Healing Powers
of the Heart*

Josefine Stark

*with Christine Meiner, Boyd Badten
and Shanti Hee*

StarkLight Press
BOZEMAN, MONTANA

Kuan Yin's Miracle Mantras:
Awakening the Healing Powers of the Heart

ISBN: 978-0-9831534-2-9

E-book (PDF download) version available at
www.KuanYinsMiracleMantras.com
$9.99

Photo credit: Water image in Chapter 10 is
copyright © 2002 by Alexander Lauterwasser,
from Water Sound Images,
MACROmedia Publishing,
Newmarket, NH.
www.cymaticsource.com
Thank you, Jeff Volk.

Photo credit: Chinese clerical script in
Chapter 18 is copyright © 2003
by Andrew Owen from
*Xin Jing—Heart Sutra, A New Translation
from the Chinese Version*

Cover photo: The statue of Kuan Yin holding
the Sutras stands at the Nanshan Temple
in Sanya, Hainan Island, China. There are
actually two statues of Kuan Yin back-to-back.
On the opposite side, she holds mala beads
for the giving of mantras. Both are over 350 feet tall,
taller than the Statue of Liberty.

Published by StarkLight Press™
309 East Garfield Street, Suite A
Bozeman, Montana 59715

Dedication

To Mark L. Prophet,

twentieth-century mystic and messenger

for the Great Brotherhood of Light,

now the master Lanello

Kuan Yin as Lord Shiva (2006). Kuan Yin is shown performing a divine dance of creation and destruction. The surrounding flames represent the manifest Universe. The upper left hand holds fire (agni) signifying destruction. The upper right hand holds an hourglass drum (amaru) signifying creation. The stoic face of Shiva represents neutrality and balance.The second right hand shows the Abhaya mudra for protection from evil and ignorance.The second left hand points toward the lifted foot that signifies upliftment and liberation.The dance position performed is in which the universe is created, maintained and resolved. [Artist Zeng Hao, Dun Huang Art Studio, by permission, www.zhdhart.com]

Table of Contents

PART III ~ Miracle Mantras & Powerful Meditations

Acknowledgments

My profound gratitude to Jeanne House at Sol Communication, my book packager and agent, for her many excellent suggestions, moral support and cheerful can-do attitude. Sol Communication helps to illuminate the seed ideas of new luminary thought leaders on the cutting edge of science, art, spirituality, psychology and other leading communications.

I would also like to acknowledge Sidian Morningstar Jones for designing my website and providing an excellent representation of Kuan Yin, along with my practical methods to practice her qualities of compassion and forgiveness.

Huge thanks also to Christine Meiner who contributed three chapters of this book and did four years of research on Kuan Yin's thirty-three manifestations and their mantras. (It took so long because she received initiations in every mantra in each version as it evolved.) The original purpose of the book was to get this information to the public, so without her work this book could not have been written.

Special thanks to Denis Ouellette for his editing, typesetting, graphics and publishing expertise.

Also to my typist William Star and to Patrick Fernandes for additional revisions.

Much thanks to Shanti Hee for doing an all-nighter to write Chapter 18 before dashing off to the airport to fly back to Hawaii.

Heartfelt gratitude also to Boyd Badten for taking time from his busy schedule to write up his Ho'oponopono Forgiveness Meditation.

I am very grateful to Dawn Covington, Ed.D. of New Wisdom University for sharing the material on the violet light from her Pure Joy System.

Thanks to my son Andrew Leung for creating the three ink illustrations of Kuan Yin.

Gratitude to Joyce Baylor, who, after I had written half of this book and told her I was finished, paused a moment to connect with Kuan Yin, then replied, "It's supposed to be 24 or 25 chapters!"

Thanks to David Milak of the Sacred Mysteries Bookstore in Livingston, Montana, who asked me to do a Kuan Yin presentation at a lecture series, thereby getting this project started.

I'd also like to gratefully acknowledge the author Robert Simmons of *Heaven and Earth*, a crystal and jewelry store in Vermont, for his gracious permission to quote from his materials.

Special thanks to the anonymous American Buddhist monk from Berkeley, California, for his helpful comments and for correcting some of my misconceptions.

I'm grateful for Gregory Bodwell of The Summit Lighthouse for generously giving permission to quote from their publications and to use some of their violet-fire mantras.

My appreciation goes to the helpful staff at the Belgrade Library in Montana for their patient help with all my requests.

I'd like to acknowledge my beloved dog Nike, my companion and protector for almost thirteen years, who passed on during the writing of this book. I miss our long rambles together through fields and forests while I practiced wordless awareness meditation. Our walks helped me clear my mind to receive inspiration and guidance.

And most importantly, I am especially grateful to Kuan Yin for guiding me throughout this project in the bringing together of all the needed information. She has frequently come to my rescue in every area of my life.

Introduction

I was first introduced to Kuan Yin by my Chinese mother-in-law Sun Ho Leung in the early 1980s. Later she gave me a porcelain statue of Kuan Yin holding a baby when my son Andrew Leung was born in 1986. It is one of several that strangely never need dusting. My mother-in-law could not read because during her childhood in China only boys were taught reading. Yet through oral tradition, she knew many of the miracle stories attributed to Kuan Yin that were published in collections in temple gazettes.

I learned more about Kuan Yin and her mantras from The Summit Lighthouse and from John Blofeld's *Bodhisattva of Compassion*. When several books on Kuan Yin came out in the 1990s, I felt moved to write one, as I found that much was missing. Every time another Kuan Yin book was published, I secretly hoped it would save me the time and effort of writing my own. Three things in particular were always missing: 1) the teaching on the violet light; 2) many of Kuan Yin's key mantras; and 3) an explanation of the science of the power of sound. At that time, I had not yet discovered her sutras (ancient sacred texts) as they were usually missing as well, so it especially pleases me to include her most important one, *The Great Compassion Dharani Sutra*.

I did not create this information. It was gleaned from decades of research in scientific writings, and both ancient and modern spiritual books. Some of it comes from my direct experiences, and some from my various spiritual teachers. I've tried to make this book as user-friendly and as comprehensive as possible, but there is still much more material. I leave that for those who can read old manuscripts in Sanskrit or Chinese. Several times during the past year, when I thought the book was almost done, more material and information that begged to be included came to me.

A few things are probably not politically correct, but to me, truth is more important than political correctness, and these are often mutually exclusive. In our humanistic culture, people say, "You decide what's right," but this is not true. It would be more accurate to advise that you discern what's right. Right and wrong have been established throughout the universe for eons and are based on the laws of energy. We are all in training to practice right use of energy, including love, wisdom, sex, and the mastery of thought and feeling through the heart.

Modern spiritual teachers point to compassion as the new driving force in our evolution. A palpable sense of collective quickening is occurring and many feel the oncoming shift toward heart-based awareness. One of the tools to ride this wave successfully is Heartsound, a term I coined to describe what results when prayers and mantras are encoded with positive heart feelings. Those who have mastered the art of traveling into the heart during meditation say that Zero Point in the heart is both a portal to higher planes and a universal convergence point.

It has been observed that true joy comes not from pursuing ease and pleasure, but from serving life and focusing on giving, whether it be loving-kindness, knowledge, time or whatever we have to offer. In mantra and meditation practice, we connect with the flow of Divine Love in our hearts and release this scintillating energy to the world, opening the faucet of joy.

True power comes not from controlling others, but from the ability to create positive change in ourselves, our lives and our world. Modern science tells us that *all* reality is waveform patterns. This means we have the power to change our reality and can do so by changing those waveform patterns with sound vibration overlayed with feeling and intention. Kuan Yin mantra sounds are among the most powerful frequency shifters we can employ to create new realities.

Many have noted that as the cycles of time and consciousness accelerate on this planet, esoteric secrets of the ages are being revealed as needed. New information is also coming forth at an exponential rate as our evolution now seems to demand it. The mantras in this book, especially *The Great Compassion Mantra*, were particularly intended to be used in our time for the clearing of any past energies and records holding back our spiritual evolution and forward progress.

Heartsound: Getting to Zero Point

The "Zero Point in the Heart-Core" that is used often in the Heart Sutra in Chapter 18 can be a difficult concept to understand and explain. The modern mystic, Shanti Hee, frequently communes in this heart space with Kuan Yin. When she came to visit, I interviewed her for clarification. She said it was not a physical location in the heart, but rather a spiritual one.

She describes it in various ways as:

- A gateway to the unified connection point of the Universe where all-knowing, all-being and all-seeing converge

- A unified field of living energy

- A state of pure existence in the formless plane

- The Source of all form, the plane of pure, living energy prior to its expression in form: the Source Field

- A unified field of living Love where all form merges at a single point

- The Core Source from which all emanates and returns

- A unified state of all-knowingness, all-beingness and all-seeingness where there is oneness with all life and with all dimensions

- A state of joy, peace and oneness with the Source

- Inclusive of the Zero-Point Field understood by modern physics, but beyond the matter planes

So there you have it! It is simultaneously a transcendent gateway and a connection point, a vast living energy field, and convergence point for all totality, and even more so, a state of all Beingness and Knowingness. And yes, it's ALL within the human heart, in a protected, interior, spiritual plane of existence.

With my mind still reeling, I asked Shanti Hee how we access this point in the heart, and she replied, "By tone, intoning." She also spoke of soundless sound and unified sound, where all form arises and disappears as waves whose oscillations have sound beyond the range of human ears.

I asked for a simple method or technique to put in this book so readers could quickly go to Zero Point. This was not given to me because it is not yet time. There are no shortcuts on the spiritual path. The first requirements are always the mastery of the body, mind and feelings, and the refinement of consciousness whereby there can be an awakening to the awareness of the loving, unified oneness of all life. She said, "Those with true purity of heart will automatically be there in Love."

So for us at this time, love is the key to the door, but as will be explained later in this book, it must be loving feelings in the heart. Beautiful thoughts of love in the head are only fruitful when they become connected to heart feelings. And they become powerful when vocalized as Heartsound, which Shanti Hee hinted was the access code to Zero Point.

My spiritual teachers agree that millennia of negative-energy records are rapidly returning to our doorstep. With the higher dimensional frequencies of violet light that can be accessed through the prayers and mantras given here, these karmic records can be mitigated before they arrive to be dealt with in the physical. These powerful mantras can be used during personal, national and planetary crises, and better still can be used daily to avert them.

This timeless information will be just as applicable a hundred years from now as it was in centuries long past. The science of prayer and mantra crosses cultures and traditions because the cleansing of earth's records and karma is required in order for us to move forward in the new millennium. The techniques for this holy work have been given here.

If something in this book is not in agreement with your beliefs, after some just discernment within your heart, feel free to disregard it. Use only what is useful for your progress at this time. The Lord created many paths to allow for psychological and cultural differences among peoples. Some people relate to devotional paths, some to more mental approaches, others to physical works, and so forth. Ultimately they all converge at the same goal—union with the Divine.

This book is for those who desire to discover more about Kuan Yin and to develop an intimate connection with her. Also, those who wish to understand the practical applications of prayer and mantra for resolving life's challenges will find many useful tools here. The mantras are for people of all faiths, and the information in these pages is also a valuable aid for anyone desiring to develop greater love, compassion and unity consciousness as exemplified by Kuan Yin's spiritual mission. And, of course, this book is for anyone who could use a few miracles!

Kuan Yin delivered The Great Compassion Mantra millennia ago so that "living beings may obtain peace and joy, be healed of illness, enjoy prosperity, erase past sins and offenses, remove hardship and suffering, and increase spiritual attainment and virtue." She said, "The blessings, virtues and karmic repayments accruing to those who recite and hold this mantra are inconceivable... They are beacons of light to the world... Use this mantra to rescue living beings and heal diseases."

This manuscript was written in front of a large statue of Kuan Yin on my writing table and I continually felt guided regarding her wishes for this book. She is the one who gave me the word Heartsound to describe these mantra practices. Whatever your material or spiritual needs and desires, the tools in this book and moreover Kuan Yin herself will help you.

Josefine Stark
Bozeman, Montana, 2011

~ PART I ~
The Essence of Divine Compassion

Kuan Yin
of the Willow Branch

CHAPTER 1 ~ **Who Is Kuan Yin?**

Kuan Yin and her story, legends and miracles are well known in most of Asia. The Western traveler who sees her image in statues and paintings throughout the Orient often wonders about this revered and popular figure.

Her Names

Her short Chinese name as Kuan Yin means "Hearer of Sounds" and her full name *Kuan Shih Yin* means "Hearer of the World's Sounds." According to Eastern tradition, when Kuan Yin was about to enter heaven and stood on the threshold, she heard the cries of distress coming from the world and turned back to help all who suffer in the earth plane. The term "hearer" of sound can also be translated as "perceiver" or "regarder" of the world's sounds.

She is known in much of Asia as a divine emanation that answers the prayers of those who faithfully call upon her name. She removes obstacles, erases past offenses, dispenses mercy, healing and spiritual graces, while always meeting the true inner needs of the soul.

One of her many titles is *Bodhisattva of Compassion*. The word Bodhisattva comes from the Sanskrit "bodhi," meaning enlightenment. The term usually denotes an enlightened or awakened being who has vowed to forgo higher realms and full liberation in order to save and assist those still struggling in the physical world. A Bodhisattva cultivates virtue and pursues his/her spiritual career while on a path of self-sacrifice for the welfare of others and gives compassionate, loving service to humanity and to all sentient life. A Bodhisattva (*P'u Sa* in Chinese) can be an unascended person still in embodiment on the earth or a celestial being like Kuan Yin. At this highest transcendent level the title is *Mahasattva*.

Kuan Yin is a cross-cultural, non-denominational figure revered by many spiritual and religious traditions around the world. She serves the aspirants of all spiritual heritages and paths. Those who espouse a concept of an impersonal formless divinity see her as an expression of the *essence* of compassion, or as a symbol of it. Others who acknowledge a personal Godhead view her as a divine embodiment of this virtue. Some view her as both the impersonal and personal manifestations of divine compassion, with no contradiction. She nurtures the growth of this quality in us through our devotions and our interpersonal relationships with others.

Kuan Yin has been revered in China for over 2,000 years, and she is known by different names around the world. Her Cantonese name is *Kwoon Yam*. Other variations of her name include *Quan Am* in Vietnamese, *Kwanse'um* in Korean, *Kanin* in Balinese, and *Kwannon* or *Kannon* in Japanese. The Japanese corporation Canon derived its name from hers. The various spellings of her name include *Kwan Yin*, *Gwan Yin* or *Guan Yin*, as these approximate the Chinese pronunciation. Frequently she is called *Kuan Tzu Tsai* or *Guan Zhi Zai* (pronounced *gwun zuh zy*), which means Master Perceiver or Observer of the Ultimate Nature of Things. In Tibet, she is known in the male form as *Chenresig*, and in the female form as *Tara*.

In the past, she had a number of other appellations including *Kuan Shih Nien*, Perceiver of the World's Thoughts, and *Kuan Shih Yeh*, Perceiver of Karma, but these have fallen into non-use through the centuries.

Her Titles

Kuan Yin is also referred to as The Goddess of Mercy, meaning she is a celestial embodiment of the Divine quality of mercy. The titles of god or goddess are not meant to imply there is more than the One God who said, "Beside me there is no other." [Isaiah 44:6] These titles are given to ascended and cosmic beings who by their attainment and mastery embody one or more of the various aspects or qualities of the Divine. In the tradition of the Great Brotherhood of Light, a cosmic hierarchy serving mankind known in the Bible as the "saints robed in white," Kuan Yin is an ascended lady master. She upholds her role as The Goddess of Mercy by serving on the Karmic Board, comprised of masters who oversee the balancing of karma for the earth and her evolutions.

In Japan, Kuan Yin has the title of Buddha, and in other places in the East, she is known as the Buddha Mary or Madonna. A Buddha is not a god but one who has reached the highest level of enlightenment and is awakened to the true divine nature of everything. She is known around the world as the compassionate savioress and is a role model for all who want to emulate her on their spiritual path.

Esoteric teachers say that Mary and Kuan Yin often work together. They ensoul the cosmic principle of Mother, which is nurturing and life-giving.

Historical Origins

The name *Kuan Shih Yin* came from the Chinese translation of *Avalokitesvara* (*AH-vahl-lo KEET-ess-SHVAH-rah*), which in Sanskrit means, "The Lord who hearkens to the cries of the world." Avalokitesvara (sometimes *Avalokita* for short) is a male celestial being, the *Bodhisattva of Compassion*. Isvara (*Eesh-VAH-ra*) is a Sanskrit suffix meaning Lord. In early Chinese iconography, up to about 700 CE, Kuan Yin is shown as either an androgynous or a male figure, often complete with mustache. The feminization of her images started after this time and was completed between 900 and 1,200 CE.

Avalokitesvara has been venerated in India for over 2,000 years. The practice of invoking him was brought to China by missionary monks and other travelers as early as the first century. When ancient texts such as the Lotus Sutra were translated into Chinese, during the first few hundred years of the common era, the name of Avalokitesvara was always translated as Kuan Shih Yin, and remained a male figure for centuries.

He is frequently depicted with a thousand arms and eyes, sometimes with an eye in the palm of each hand, and often with eleven heads. This is a metaphorical portrayal as in this form he sees in all directions, senses the burdens of all mankind, and has innumerable hands to alleviate suffering and hardship.

But what is the origin of Avalokitesvara? According to Indian sutras, he was born from a ray of light that came from the Amitabha Buddha's right eye. Legend has it that he came forth bearing a lotus flower, and his first words were, *Om Mani Padme Hum* ("Behold! The Jewel in the Lotus"). This genesis is a metaphorical way of saying that the Amitabha Buddha ensouls the primary energy of compassion and Avalokitesvara embodies the secondary essence. Amitabha, whose name means "Infinite Light," is the Dhyani Buddha of wisdom, the wisdom that sees every being as an expression of the One. His image can often be found on Kuan Yin's head within her topknot. Dhyani buddhas are transcendent celestial beings often seen by devotees in meditation. Amitabha is revered from India to Japan. He is also known as *Amitayus*, *Amida*, and *Amit'o Fo*.

Her Mantra

The **Om Mani Padme Hum** is found written in two different ways in and on prayer wheels, on jewelry, etc.: in Tibetan script (top) and the ancient Indian Ranjana script.

In the 8th century AD, the knowledge of Avalokitesvara spread to Tibet with the introduction there of Buddhism by Padma Sambhava. As the Bodhisattva of Compassion, Avalokitesvara (Chenresig in Tibetan) and his mantra, *Om Mani Padme Hum*, quickly achieved wide popularity there. The Tibetan version of this mantra is "*Om Mani Peme Hung*," pronounced "*ohm MAH-nee BAY-may hung.*"

Om Mani Padme Hum is often called the mani mantra or the six syllables. *Mani* means jewel; *padme* means lotus. The jewel can refer to Avalokitesvara's presence in the heart, to Kuan Yin, or to the Divine Presence in the heart of the devotee. Chanting this mantra is an effective tool for generating compassion. The *Om* at the beginning of many mantras is the primordial sound essence of the universe from which all creation manifested. Chanting it leads to an experience of universality and non-duality. *Hum* always comes at the end and represents the universal in the individual heart, the infinite within the finite, thus completing the circle. In *Mantra Meditation*, Thomas Ashley-Farrand writes that this mantra "is the most often chanted mantra in the world. Pulling energy from the lower chakras to the upper ones, it activates these centers and circulates energy around them so that the energy in the subtle body becomes centered in the upper body. When this mantra is chanted by anyone, all humanity is benefited."

Lama Zopa Rinpoche says, "The benefits of reciting *Om Mani Padme Hum* are like the infinite sky. Depending on how perfectly qualified one's mind is and on one's motivation, even reciting *Om Mani Padme Hum* one time can purify negative karma [offenses, sins, misused energy remaining as a debt to life]. For example, a fully ordained monk who has received all four defeats [i.e., breaking his vows by engaging in sex, theft, murder and lying about his spiritual attainment] can completely purify that very heavy negative karma by reciting *Om Mani Padme Hum*... The benefits are so many that the explanations will never finish... If one recites *Om Mani Padme Hum* one thousand times every day, then one's children up to seven generations will not be reborn in the lower realms... [If that one] goes in water, into a river or ocean, the water becomes blessed."

This mantra also blesses our ancestors to seven generations back. One thousand repetitions takes about twenty minutes. Some people recite it all day as they work or when they drive.

Avalokitesvara and Kuan Yin are the same being. Avalokitesvara is the male aspect with the Indian name and Kuan Yin is the female *shakti* or power aspect with her Chinese name, so these names can be used interchangeably in our spiritual work.

Tara

Another Tibetan embodiment of compassion is known as Tara (also called Dolma) who manifests herself in twenty-one different forms in order to help suffering beings. There are numerous miracle stories of people being rescued from danger by one of her appearances, usually in the form of a sixteen-year-old, fun-loving girl.

This is where scholars think the Chinese feminization of Kuan Yin began. Many Chinese could not relate to some of India's seemingly bizarre depictions of Avalokitesvara with eleven heads and a thousand arms, but they could relate to Tara's lovely image of compassion. The early feminized Chinese depictions of Kuan Yin incorporated the postures and hand gestures of Tara.

Tara is now usually considered to be an emanation of Kuan Yin by devotees in the West. Spiritual beings can create emanations of themselves by dividing in two, who then each in turn also divide in two and so forth. The

Tibetans call to twenty-one aspects of Tara, each associated with a color and an aspect of intercession, the two principle ones being the White Tara and the Green Tara. Two of the most popular mantras to Tara are:

Om Tam Taraaye Namaha

[Ohm tum TAH-ray-ay NAH-mah-hah]

and

Om Tare Tuttare Ture svaha

[Ohm TAH-ray to-TAH-ray TOO-ray shva-HA]

Her seed-essence syllable is *TAM*. Kuan Yin's seed essence syllable is *HRIH*, and her mantra is *Om Mani Padme Hum*. A spiritual being's seed syllable has the same energetic frequency as that being. It is the key sound that can evoke their energy when focused on devoutly.

His Holiness the Dalai Lama is also considered by some to be an incarnation and emanation of Avalokitesvara or Tara. However, from a spiritual viewpoint, gender attributed to a celestial being is unimportant as beings in higher dimensions are basically androgynous. In the highest, formless planes they are beyond the male/female duality. The following diagram is a recapitulation of the lineage.

AMITABHA
A cosmic being ensouling the primary essence of compassion who sent a ray of light to form...

AVALOKITESVARA (CHENRESIG)
who is the secondary essence of compassion...

KUAN YIN
the female aspect (*shakti*) of Avalokitesvara...

TARA
the emanation of Kuan Yin or Avalokitesvara, depending on your viewpoint.

CHAPTER 2 ~ **Famous Embodiments & Legends**

Traditional scriptures reveal that eons ago, Avalokitesvara attained the status of a buddha, a fully enlightened or awakened being. In the Great Brotherhood of Light tradition, Kuan Yin ascended many thousands of years ago from an ancient Chinese civilization that predates recorded history. She has occasionally taken embodiment to awaken mankind to greater kindness and mercy.

Miao Shan

One of these incarnations was that of Princess Miao Shan. (There are numerous versions of her story.) She was the youngest of three daughters born to a king. Because he had no sons, he wanted all three girls to be married to princes to increase the likelihood of getting a grandson to inherit his kingdom. When she reached her teenage years, Miao Shan refused to marry and begged to be allowed to live in a convent. The king agreed, thinking she would soon tire of the difficult life and come back home. However, she remained content in the convent and the king tried an increasing series of harsh and horrible measures to get her to return home. His anger increased with each attempt. Finally, he had her imprisoned and she was given only the most revolting food. And still she would not consent to be married.

In his rage, the king ordered his soldiers to kill her. As the executioner raised his sword, it shattered to pieces. A great storm immediately arose and an enormous white tiger bounded in and carried her away to a cave in the hills. Here a buddha appeared and told her to seek safety on P'ut'o Island where she could meditate night and day.

So Miao Shan spent the next nine years on the island meditating and doing many deeds of compassion for the inhabitants. It was during this time that her two young assistants (seen by her side in paintings and statues) entered her service. They are Shan Tsai, a boy, and Lung Nu, a girl.

Eventually, her father the king became terminally ill. A monk appeared at the royal court and told the king that only the hands and eyes of a person who had never experienced hatred or anger could heal him. The monk also told him that such a being lived on P'u-t'o Island. The king's messenger was sent to the island where he found Miao Shan. When she heard his story, she immediately pulled out her eyes and cut off her hands to be made into medicine.

After the king recovered, he and the queen decided to go to thank the person who had so selflessly donated vital body parts for his healing. When they entered the cave where she lived, they discovered to their horror that it was their youngest daughter. She then assumed her celestial form amid a rain of flowers. Her parents converted to the spiritual path and built a shrine in that place. The area is now called Fragrant Mountain.

According to the Chinese lunar calendar, Kuan Yin's birthday is celebrated on the nineteenth day of the second month, which is Miao Shan's birthday. The nineteenth day of the sixth month is a festival day honoring her enlightenment, and the nineteenth day of the ninth month traditionally celebrates her ordination.

Governor's Daughter

In another old story, Kuan Yin was born as the only daughter of a provincial governor. She was raised in a mansion and daily gazed at a monastery on the nearby hill. She longed to go there but was always refused permission, and no one mentioned its bad reputation to her. One day, she sneaked away from her home and went up to the monastery.

Once inside, seeing beautiful statues and hearing sacred songs, she thought it must be the dwelling place of saintly people, but she was wrong. As she wandered through the halls she was abducted into a darkened room.

Meanwhile the governor had searched everywhere for his daughter. Servants who checked at the monastery were told she wasn't there. Her father was sure she was, but it never occurred to him that she was being held against her will. He assumed she voluntarily remained there, having liaisons with the monks. Because of this disgrace to his family, he had his soldiers set fire to the monastery and burned it to the ground along with all who were inside. Saving face had been more important to him than his child's life.

The next day, the governor was in his garden when the figure of his daughter appeared. She said, "Father, you had no mercy on me, an innocent girl, so you must now remain childless. Heaven saw my undeserved suffering and elevated me. From now on, it will be my work to comfort and rescue."

Most of the legends regarding Kuan Yin's embodiments have a similar theme—birth as a daughter to a noble family, refusal to be married, entry in a convent, being harshly treated, and preferring to suffer a cruel death rather than be used for impure purposes. She made a vow of chastity eons ago in order to maintain her power of alleviating the suffering of others.

Thi Kinh

In Vietnam, Kuan Yin is believed to have incarnated as Thi Kinh. To repay a monetary debt, Thi Kinh's father gave her to a wealthy family to be a wife for their son. After they were married, the son was disappointed that they remained childless. One day as she was mending clothes, she looked at her sleeping husband and noticed a long hair growing from a mole on his chest. As she was snipping it with her scissors, he woke up and angrily accused her of attempted murder. He wanted an excuse to marry someone else in hopes of getting a son.

Thi Kinh was thrown out and the entire village believed her to be guilty. With no other way to survive, she shaved her head to look like a man and went to live as a monk at a Buddhist temple.

Sometime later a village girl saw "him" in the street and fell in love. One dark night, a man appeared outside this girl's window. She thought it was the monk, so she let him in and they slept together. After her pregnancy became obvious, she told her livid father that it was the monk's doing. Thi Kinh was cruelly treated once again when the villagers heard the story. She was told to leave the temple and so had to live in the streets.

The entire community abused her, yet she kept her silence on proving her innocence in order not to humiliate the girl. As a monk, she had taken vows of compassion and she took them seriously.

When the girl's baby was born it was given to Thi Kinh. Everywhere she traveled with the child to beg for milk she was ill-treated for shaming the monastery. One day she was savagely beaten to death and the baby was given to a temple.

The truth finally came out when she was disrobed for burial washing. As a woman, she could not have been the father of the child, yet she had endured horrendous suffering to shield the baby's mother from public shame. As the spirit of Kuan Yin, she became the role model for great compassion displayed by Vietnamese women to this day.

Pao-Chih

Kuan Yin sometimes appears to people as a monk and has had several embodiments as a "divine monk." One of these is believed to be Pao-chih (AD 425–514). He was known for his eccentric behavior and long hair. A pair of scissors and a mirror hung from his staff, though historians do not know the symbolism of this.

He often went for days without eating. He occasionally ate fish (forbidden for a monk), yet afterwards the fish would be found swimming in its bowl again. He was able to bilocate and predict the future.

Pao-chih purportedly wrote some of the Buddhist rituals such as the "Water-Land Rite," a long ritual for funerals. In one Chinese work, thirty-six poems are attributed to him, including fourteen that describe the different types of non-duality. On two occasions he reportedly pulled off his face to reveal the face of Kuan Yin but this may be a historical embellishment.

In her many incarnations, Kuan Yin often defies convention to teach people to look beyond the superficial into the spiritual, and most especially she comes to illustrate the way of kindness toward all living beings.

CHAPTER 3 ~ **Kuan Yin's Island & Her Etheric Retreat**

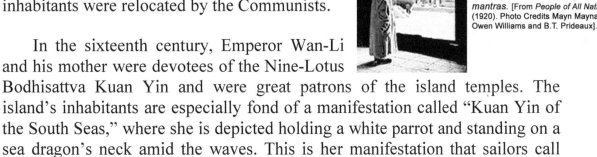

T he international pilgrimage site of P'u-to' Shan Island is actually a mountain emerging from the ocean in the Chusan Archipelago off the coast of China near Ningpo. It lies in the traditional trade route to Japan and Korea. This beautiful, hilly island is only about 8.5 miles long by 3.5 miles wide and shaped like an open-mouthed dragon's head. Some call it the place where the Bodhisativa lives. Many believe it to be the location of Kuan Yin's palace of Mount Potalaka, the setting of the Dharani Sutra.

Over the centuries, monasteries have been built there, destroyed and rebuilt. Over 300 temples were ruined in the sixteenth century alone. Most temples were destroyed again during the Chinese Cultural Revolution and their inhabitants were relocated by the Communists.

P'u-t'o Shan Island. Until the Chinese Cultural Revolution when most temples were destroyed, many monasteries splendid with gilded images and carvings studded this holy island, once wholly devoted to the culture of Buddha. Here in many latticed shrines, yellow-robed monks once passed their idyllic lives chanting the sacred mantras. [From People of All Nations (1920). Photo Credits Mayn Maynard Owen Williams and B.T. Prideaux].

In the sixteenth century, Emperor Wan-Li and his mother were devotees of the Nine-Lotus Bodhisattva Kuan Yin and were great patrons of the island temples. The island's inhabitants are especially fond of a manifestation called "Kuan Yin of the South Seas," where she is depicted holding a white parrot and standing on a sea dragon's neck amid the waves. This is her manifestation that sailors call upon for rescue.

P'u-t'o is renowned as a place of miracles. Kuan Yin's appearances are known to have occurred in the Cave of Tidal Sounds (with its sometimes deafening roars) and other nearby auspicious areas, like Parrot Stone and Sudana's Rock. Many devotees have been blessed with divine contact in these and other locations. Miraculous sightings have made this island popular for over a thousand years.

In AD 916, a Japanese monk named Egaku was taking a statue of Kuan Yin from China to Japan when his boat got stuck near the west side of P'u-t'o. He prayed to Kuan Yin, promising to follow her direction and build a temple. Then the boat began moving and eventually stopped at the Cave of Tidal Sounds. He left the statue there and a local person built a shrine for it.

The statue was eventually returned to a monastery on the mainland. Afterwards a pilgrim came to P'u-t'o and carved another image. He completed his work in only thirty days, then disappeared. He is believed to have been Kuan Yin.

In the eleventh century, Wang Shun-feng's boat got caught in a violent storm. The boat was unable to move when a huge sea turtle became trapped underneath it. Terrified, Shun-feng faced the Cave of Tidal Sounds and prayed. Suddenly, Kuan Yin appeared from the cave in a burst of light and the turtle disappeared. His boat could move again.

In another old testimonial, sailors drifted in the area for several days. The sky was dark and overcast day and night and they were unable to get their bearings. The sailors turned to the distant island and prayed. Then a light blazed and filled the area like the brightest daylight and they were able to see the way to their destination.

Many of the divine apparitions to pilgrims occur in or near the Cave of Tidal Sounds, often accompanied by a brilliant light. The Bodhisattva sometimes appears clothed in purple and has a lavender cast to her skin. She frequently wears a white robe. Her favored position is a seated posture called Royal Ease, her right arm extended and resting on her raised right knee.

On P'u-t'o, the Cave of Brahma's Voice has also attracted many pilgrims, but unfortunately, some committed suicide there in hopes of ending their sufferings and going to paradise. Divine law opposes such activity and heavy spiritual consequences ensue, not as punishment, but to teach and correct the errant soul. Even so, there have been a number of reports of Kuan Yin's apparitions at the Cave of Brahma's Voice and devotees continue to flock to both these famous caves.

Many people come to this island in the springtime for the celebration of Kuan Yin's birthday. Over 100,000 people sometimes arrive for this occasion, frequently in April according to the Chinese calendar. About one million people visit during the course of a year, and sincere devotees feel her presence tangibly on this island in spite of the bars and brothels that have been established there.

The Temple of Mercy, Kuan Yin's Etheric Retreat

According to esoteric teachings, there are fourteen etheric retreats and cities located in a dimensional plane just above the physical. Many spiritual retreats in this octave radiate lines of energy that connect to each other. They also radiate spiritual light to the earth. Celestial beings and masters use these retreats as their earthly homes and also to anchor and emanate energies. Some contain libraries of ancient records, while others are schools of instruction and training that our souls can attend at night while we sleep.

Some who have consciously remembered their retreat experiences when they awaken in the morning have provided us with descriptions. Most of us forget. Occasionally we may remember just a phrase of a teaching that stays with us during the day. However, our soul remembers all the instructions and the conscious mind receives it as needed. Unfortunately, because of humanity's indulgence in their lower nature and the downward vibration of most of the music and entertainment in our popular culture, most people travel at night to a lower astral dimension, which is the realm of delusion and darkness—the underworld, the abode of entities and demons.

True etheric retreats and cities are places of extraordinary light and beauty. "Etheric" does not mean "ethereal." In this plane, everything seems even more solid and real than our so-called physical plane. A few retreats are inside some of the mountains of our planet, such as within the Grand Tetons in Wyoming. Several people have told me that they remember returning in the morning from the underground retreat at Luxor in Egypt.

Kuan Yin's retreat in the etheric plane is near the foothills of Beijing in China. Called the Temple of Mercy, it has a circle of twelve pagodas with a taller, thirteenth pagoda in the middle. This multi-storied building is topped by a golden dome. The middle pagoda contains many classrooms and meeting rooms where souls may go at night to study or attend lectures. There's also a central altar where the pinkish-violet mercy flame burns continuously in a golden vessel.

The grounds are landscaped with huge crystals, jeweled-lotus pools, waterfalls, fountains, lush foliage and flowers. The heady fragrance of lilacs and lotus blossoms wafts on a gentle celestial breeze. Before falling asleep at night, those who wish to visit Kuan Yin's retreat can ask the angels to guide them safely there and back.

It is a sad irony that the Temple of Mercy is located in a land of much brutal cruelty toward animals, children, prisoners, Tibetans, Christians and many others. Perhaps it is here because this is where it is most desperately needed.

Kuan Yin's personal love gives healing and renewed hope to all who come to her retreat. She multiplies her presence to attend to everyone who calls on her. All ascended and cosmic beings and the angelic hosts can multiply their presence. This is sometimes called their electronic presence, and it enables them to be in many places around the world at the same time. If a million people call to Archangel Michael for protection, he overshadows each person. Clairvoyants can often see this overshadowing by spiritual beings.

You can ask Kuan Yin to place her electronic presence over you or anyone else to receive her blessings and assistance with the resolution of problems.

CHAPTER 4 ~ **Kuan Yin's Sutra Promises**

The Kuan Yin Sutra is the name given to the 25th chapter of the Lotus Sutra when this chapter is published on its own. (In some translations, it may be numbered as Chapter 23 or 24.) It is widely recited and memorized throughout the orient.

Kuan Yin devotees at a shrine in China.

The origin of the Lotus Sutra is unknown, but it is assumed to be from India or Central Asia. The first Chinese translation was made in 255 CE, so we know it was in existence long before then. The monk Kumarajiva, a scholar and seer, wrote his famous, classical Chinese translation around 406 CE. Of the many different translations and versions, his is the most popular and has been recited since that time.

The full title of Chapter 25 is "The Universal Gateway of the Bodhisattva Who Regards the World's Sounds," but it is usually just referred to as The Universal Gateway. This chapter enumerates the benefits and miraculous help bestowed when one mindfully calls upon the name of this Bodhisattva and reverently holds on to it in situations of suffering or danger. It does not matter in which language the name is pronounced.

33

The following is a summary of the promises given, drawn from various Chinese and Sanskrit translations of this sutra:

- One will not be harmed if in a great fire.

- One will be saved if carried off in a raging flooded river.

- If even one person calls on the name of the Bodhisattva, when on a treasure ship blown off course to a land of evildoers, all on the ship will be saved.

- A person who calls on the name when under imminent attack with weapons will be delivered.

- Tormenting spirits and devils are unable to harm anyone they hear calling the name.

- A prisoner who sincerely calls the name will be freed.

- Travelling merchants, being attacked by bandits, will be delivered if they chant in unison "Hail to the Bodhisattva who Regards the World's Sounds."

- Those beset by addictions to lust and other cravings can lose their desires if they think of this Bodhisattva with constant reverence, imploring her aid.

- Likewise, those with anger, hatred or ignorance can rid themselves of these if they keep reverence to her in their minds.

- Because of the great power and authority of Kuan Shih Yin to confer benefits, all living beings should remain mindful of her.

- A woman desiring a son and venerating Kuan Yin will bear a son of wisdom and virtue. If she wants a daughter she will bear a lovely girl of virtue, respected by many.

- For those who respect and honor this Bodhisattva, good fortune will not be fleeting. Thus all beings should accept and hold to the name Kuan Shih Yin [or Avalokitesvara] and venerate this compassionate aspect of the Godhead, no matter which spiritual path they are on.

- For one who accepts, upholds and cherishes the name of this Bodhisattva and even just once offers obeisances to her and gives alms in her name, his good fortune will never be exhausted and he will attain great merit and virtue. The benefits of cherishing this name are immense.

- If a supplicant needs someone to come in the body of a Buddha in order to be saved, Kuan Yin will manifest in a Buddha body and preach the Teaching for them. In no matter what form a being needs someone to come to them and preach the Teaching, Kuan Yin will do it, regardless of whether it's in the form of a great celestial being, earthly king, rich man, householder, monk, saint, nun, lay person, wife, young boy or girl, dragon, nature spirit or other non-human being.

- The Perceiver of the World's Sounds travels about the earth in an variety of forms saving living beings and giving courage and safety to those in fearful or difficult circumstances.

- Chant and cherish her name and constantly remain mindful of her, for she can erase the pain of existence. She has accomplished this vow through many ages.

- If someone knocks you into a fire, think of Kuan Shih Yin's power and be saved.

- If your ship capsizes in the ocean, think of Kuan Shih Yin's saving power.

- If pushed off Mount Meru, think of Kuan Shih Yin's power.

- If pursued by criminals, think on Kuan Shih Yin's power.

- If surrounded by knife-wielding thugs, think on Kuan Shih Yin's power, that they may have compassion.

- If having problems with the law, or imprisoned, think on Kuan Shih Yin's power, and all will go well.

- If someone attempts to hurt you with hexes, black magic, poison potions, etc., think on Kuan Shih Yin's power, and the evil will return to its sender.

- If you encounter devils, entities or evil spirits, think on Kuan Shih Yin's power and they will dare not harm you.

- If you encounter wild beasts, snakes or other poisonous creatures, think on Kuan Shih Yin's power and they will retreat on hearing your voice and lose their poison.

- If dangerous storms threaten you, think on Kuan Shih Yin's power and you will be safe.

- If living beings are weighed down by great weariness, danger and suffering, the power of Kuan Shih Yin's wisdom can alleviate these.

- She beholds all creatures. There is no area of land where she does not manifest. Bit by bit, with her vast skill and knowledge, she erases the suffering of birth, old age, sickness, death and the evil circumstances in hellish astral realms.

- Continually and reverently look to her lovely face and her beautiful luminous eyes of great wisdom and compassion. Her vast pure light dispels darkness like a sun. She calms the winds and fires of misfortune, enlightening the world.

- She dispenses her "sweet dew," the Dharma Rain, to put out the fire of earthly desires.

- Whether threatened by lawsuits, armies or other dangers, think on Kuan Shih Yin's power for hatred to be dissolved and evildoers vanquished.

- Never doubt! She can offer help to all who suffer, all in danger of death. She views all with compassionate eyes. The ocean of her accumulated blessings is infinitely vast, thus humbly bow your head in reverence.

~ Part II ~
Tools for Accelerating Consciousness

Kuan Yin
of the Dragon Head

CHAPTER 5 ~ **The Power of Mercy & Compassion**

Beside the giving of her mantras with sincere devotion, the surest way to obtain the miraculous intercession of Kuan Yin or Tara is to develop a compassionate heart for all of life. As many spiritual aspirants have noted, words and deeds of great love and kindness always get the attention of heaven like nothing else can.

Divine Love

There is a difference between divine and human love. My Swedish friend Jan Hjalmarsson recently explained it this way: "True expressions of love may actually seem unloving on the surface. This is one of the differences between divine and human love. Human love has a comfortable, rosy, idealized image of how love should be, but it is conditional and hides from unpleasant realities. Divine love is unconditional. It uplifts and helps life transcend itself. It doesn't fit into the human image of love because the human avoids and omits the unpleasant or difficult learning aspects."

Love

What is the difference between love and compassion? The Apostle Paul says that love is "the fulfillment of the whole of the Law." The ascended masters, those saints and mystics whose spiritual attainment raised them to higher realms, have taught that love is the way, the key and the answer. It has been recognized as the greatest power in the world and has been called the currency of the Universe. Much more than a mental concept, love is a feeling that can be generated without limit in the heart. The masters tell us that the world's darkness can be burned up in the lovefires of the heart, meaning that the low frequencies of the energies of darkness can be annihilated by the higher frequencies of heart-core feelings. Denser frequencies are vibrationally altered and transformed into the higher frequency. In this way, the heart is used as a transformer.

Compassion

Compassion is a way of being and of how we relate to all of life. It is the *application* of the power of love. Love is not manifested when it remains in the mental realm as a concept. Several eastern traditions incorporate a *metta* (loving kindness) meditation where the practitioner generates love in the heart and projects it out for the healing of all people in the world. Some monks spend their entire lives in caves immersed in this meditation, which is true compassion because love's power is being applied.

Smithsonite

Compassion is the practical application of love expressed in actions and words to lighten the load of others and relieve suffering wherever it is found. It can be expressed by visiting a difficult one, weeding someone's garden, comforting an animal, picking up trash by the wayside to beautify it for others, or giving uplifting words of praise and encouragement. As a friend recently said, "There are only two paths in life—giving to self or giving to others." Sometimes it's a blurry line between the two and we may rationalize that we are doing for others when we are really serving our own agenda. Compassion has become the new driving evolutionary force in human consciousness.

Robert Simmons, author of *Stones of the New Consciousness*, says that the crystal Smithsonite "resonates with the vibration of Kuan Yin," and can help amplify the frequency of compassion in our hearts. He also recommends Lavender Jade for attuning with her.

John Blofeld tells the story of Jigme, a Tibetan trader, who was aided by Tara's physical appearance on four different occasions. The people of Jigme's hometown always wondered what extraordinary deed of compassion he must have performed in the past in order to merit so many divine visitations.

Forgiveness & Mercy

Someone once made the wry observation that we all want mercy for ourselves, but justice for everyone else. It's interesting that the ancient Hebrew Kabbalah texts reveal that evil began when justice became more important than mercy. The terms mercy and forgiveness are interchangeable. Dictionary definitions for mercy include:

- Forgiveness

- Willingness to let go

- Kind or compassionate treatment of an offender

- A disposition to be kind, forgiving or helpful

The definitions given for the verb to forgive include:

- To pardon

- To cease to blame or feel resentment toward

- To excuse

- To free from guilt or obligation

Television talk-show host Oprah Winfrey said, "To forgive is to forget. If you haven't forgotten, you haven't forgiven."

Crystal expert Robert Simmons says, "Celestite is the quintessential stone of forgiveness... The power of forgiveness is one of the strongest energies for healing and Celestite emanates the currents of forgiveness perhaps more than any other

Celestite

stone." Holding a Celestite stone while doing a forgiveness prayer or meditation enables our energy to lock into the crystal's energetic frequency that resonates with the vibration of forgiveness.

But why should you forgive someone? If you think of forgiveness as being an undeserved favor extended to another, it makes no sense. There's no point to it if you still see your fellow brother or sister on the path as a sinner, as deserving of punishment, as unworthy, or as lesser than yourself. Instead of seeing anyone (including yourself) as a sinner deserving punishment, see that one as a child of the Divine who makes mistakes and is capable of self-correction.

So who is your neighbor, your brother or sister? Christ taught us to pray to Our Father. What does this imply? That only God's sons and daughters, His progeny, can say to Him, "Dad." The Aramaic Abba is used for the close intimacy between parents and children and actually translates more accurately to Dad rather than the formal Father.

A *Course in Miracles* says, "See your brother as sinless... Before your brother's holiness, the world is still... Your brother's body shows not the Christ to you... Choose then, his body or his holiness as what you want to see." This is also reflected in the biblical phrase, "See no man after the flesh."

Do not look on others as guilty sinners, but only as sons of God at school here on this planet, learning lessons through practice and by making mistakes. Royalty send their sons and daughters to the best, most rigorous schools; likewise, God does the same with us. The physical universe is an educational vehicle for spiritual beings—and currently appears to have an accelerated curriculum!

All Are Part of the Divine

In *The I Am Discourses, Vol. 3*, Saint Germain said, "God can only act through the mind of His individualizations, which are clothed in the personalities you see about you. These personalities are but vehicles of use and expression of this Mighty Individuality which is God's."

The mystic Omraam Mikhaël Aïvanhov taught that, "Our Higher Self is none other than God. That is why at the highest level we are God Himself, for apart from God, there is nothing. God manifests Himself through creation and through each one of His creatures." Think about it— there is no other way He could manifest except through His creation.

This means that all compassion that we extend to one another, we literally extend to the Divine as well. The forgiveness and compassion we give to ourselves, we give to the Divine. Kuan Yin gives mercy to all of life because all of life is God. You are God in the same way that a drop of water in the ocean is the ocean. A drop of water is not the entire ocean but it is the ocean nonetheless. It is not your ego or your personality that is God, but your Higher Self or Spirit using these lower vehicles to express its consciousness and evolve in this world of form.

Every one you see is an expression of God's energy and awareness in the material universe. What an amazing concept! Every one is a manifestation of the Infinite One. Truly understand what this means whenever you look at another and joy will flood your being spontaneously, bubbling over with bliss at the realization of this cosmic secret.

Some wonder whether it is scriptural, or perhaps even heresy, to consider oneself or others as a god. When the Scribes and Pharisees, who were the political correctness police of their time, were going to stone Jesus for blasphemy, for daring to call himself a Son of God [John 10:28-34], he answered by saying that He is the one who gives eternal life and that He and the Father are one. He then referred them to a verse from the Old Testament [Psalm 82:6], replying, "Is it not written in your law, I said *ye are gods.*" His response showed that it is scripturally correct to view yourself as a Son or Daughter of God. The Psalm says, "Ye are gods and all of you are children of the Most High." The offspring of God are gods.

The Real Self—your Higher Self—is truly divine. Keeping your focus on this, rather than on the shortcomings of the outer self, makes compassion easier for yourself and others. After all, how could you not have compassion for expressions of the Divine struggling and evolving on this planet?

Kindness to All Creatures

Kuan Yin expects her devotees and everyone who requests her merciful intercession to have a loving heart towards all living beings, including animals. That is why many of her followers are vegetarians. When they recite the vow to help save all sentient life (the third of the Ten Vows, see Chapters 14 and 21), it doesn't make sense to then go out and eat of animal life. Jeffrey Masson's *The Face On Your Plate: The Truth About Food*, exposes the enormous cruelty and suffering imposed through the commercial animal-harvesting industries, including eggs and dairy production. It contains all the motivation you'll ever need to become a vegetarian!

If you want to receive compassion you have to give it. The more kindness and genuine cherishment we have for all creatures, the more merit we earn. Extending kindness to others includes eliminating our critical thoughts of them. Mentally taking people apart still counts as unkindness even when it is not expressed vocally. Even so, a truly kind person dispenses tough love when necessary. Love serves the true needs of the soul, not the outer desires of the human.

Generating Compassion

In *The 7 Secrets of Sound Healing*, author Jonathan Goldman says that the sound vibration associated with compassion is the vowel sound "ah." He recommends toning this vowel sound as a meditation while overlaying it with a feeling of love or compassion from the heart. This is what I call Heartsound. He says the "ah" sound is one of the most powerful sounds on the planet, particularly useful for generating compassion. It can be used for healing oneself or others. For planetary healing and peace, you

Vivianite

can join others toning anytime anywhere worldwide at his website, www.TempleofSacredSound.com. The frequency of the crystal Vivianite also helps us to attain and remain in a state of compassion.

How can we tell if we have a loving, compassionate heart? There's an easy way to check. Do we have a compassionate mouth? Without a compassionate mouth there is no compassionate heart. The same goes for the hands. If a person speaks with loving words, but doesn't extend himself to do the work of kindness whenever and wherever needed because it's not convenient or there isn't enough time, or for whatever reason, then there is no true compassionate heart, no matter how lovely the thoughts or words appear to be. Another reality check is the wallet test. The open heart has an open wallet; the closed heart, a closed wallet. Stinginess is incompatible with compassion. When loves remains merely an intellectual or philosophical concept, it is barren and bears no fruit.

In *The Road Less Traveled*, M. Scott Peck wrote, "A genuinely loving individual will often take loving and constructive action toward a person he or she consciously dislikes." Our greatest tests of compassion are often with those who are the most difficult to love and frequently at the most inconvenient times.

In *The Story of a Soul*, the autobiography of Saint Thérèse of Lisieux, she writes: "There is in the community a sister who has the faculty of displeasing me in everything, in her ways, her words, her character—everything seems very *disagreeable* to me. And still, she is a holy religious who must be very pleasing to God. Not wishing to give in to the natural antipathy I was experiencing, I told myself that charity must not consist in feelings but in works. Then I set myself to doing for this Sister what I would do for the person I loved the most... I wasn't content simply with praying very much for this Sister who gave me so many struggles, but I took care to render her all the services possible, and when I was tempted to answer her back in a disagreeable manner, I was content with giving her my most friendly smile and with changing the subject of the conversation."

Saint Thérèse goes on to describe the Sister's reaction: "One day at recreation, she asked in almost these words. 'Would you tell me, Sister Thérèse of the Child Jesus, what attracts you so much towards me; every time you look at me, I see you smile?' Ah! What attracted me was Jesus hidden in the depths of her soul."

Love's Work

Years ago, I had a sweet friend who was always talking about love, composing songs and poems of love and attending classes on love. She spent most of her time at church services, political meetings and social events because she "loved God and people." Yet her home was in a shambles, littered with piles of dirty laundry and dishes. Her neglected young children were usually left alone to fend for themselves. They were disheveled, unkempt, lived on cereal, and depended on school teachers for a warm jacket in Montana's severe winters. She was in love with love, but hid behind platitudes because she was "allergic" to the work of love.

Kahlil Gibran said, "And to love life through labour is to be intimate with life's inmost secret. Work is love made visible." Many people who survive a near death experience say that their entire Life Review was based on only two questions:

- Who did you love?

- Who did you serve?

This is how we evolve and earn our credits to graduate to higher dimensions.

CHAPTER 6 ~ **Connecting in the Heart with Kuan Yin & the Divine**

Many think that the way to commune with higher realms is through elevating the mind. This can never be. The spiritual dimensions are not accessible through left-brain reasoning and the Divine cannot be reached through the intellect.

Using the brain as the doorway to the non-physical planes can lead one to lower realms that are the domain of demons, entities and discarnates, some of which are only too happy to assume the guise of an angel or master. The victims of this hoax never have any idea they are receiving communications from impostors who sprinkle false teachings among true and lead many souls astray, while robbing them of their life essence.

Tanzanite

The portal to Kuan Yin (or any higher being) is through the heart. When in the frequency of love, the heart has spiritual vision. The mantra *Om Mani Padme Hum* unites the heart and mind by the union of compassion with wisdom. Those messengers who receive true dictations or other communications from saints, angels or ascended masters, do so only via the heart. The heart is able to connect with the right brain and higher dimensions through what is now often referred to as Zero Point, a multidimensional convergence point. Sometimes called *the eye of the needle*, this portal to the transcendent universe is more a state of consciousness than a physical location. The energy of the crystal Tanzanite promotes a heart-mind connection, so it is good to wear or hold during prayer or meditation.

In the pocketbook, *Access the Power of Your Higher Self*, Elizabeth Clare Prophet explains Zero Point in the heart like this: "Your attention is focused on the flame in your heart, a gift from your Presence [Higher Self]. You seem to be drawn into the light. It becomes brighter and brighter, almost blinding, and you feel as if you're being condensed into that point. All at once you pass through that point and emerge on the other side. You take a deep breath. You're floating on a sea of light."

The Institute of HeartMath® in Boulder, California,[1] which has nothing to do with math, has done an enormous amount of research on the physical heart and on emotions, validating much of the ancient mystical traditions with scientific evidence. The heart is not merely a muscle that pumps blood, it also has its own mini-brain. These are multifunctional neurons of which only a small percentage are sensitive to pulse rate, pressure, and so forth.

The heart is an intelligent system, and much more information is sent from the heart to the brain than vice versa. It responds to situations before the brain does and affects brain processing. It is the seat of wisdom and intuition. We use the brain for mental activities like balancing our checkbooks, but we need to use the heart for making decisions. The intellect, with its tendency toward arrogance, must learn to obey the heart.

Heart rate variability (the beat-to-beat change in time between beats) can be used as an indicator of connectedness with higher dimensions and wisdom. The electrocardiogram (ECG) wave-pattern is smooth and coherent when there are positive feelings like love, compassion, forgiveness, gratitude, etc. in the heart. This is referred to by the Institute of HeartMath as "being in coherence." Stress and negative feelings create a jagged wave-pattern. There are actually a couple of palm-sized biofeedback instruments available that let you know when you are in coherence. One is called the StressEraser™. They sense heart-wave fluctuations and people use them to train themselves to remain in positive-feeling states for longer periods of time. How the heartbeat is generated is still a total mystery to science.

Compassion is the emotion that most efficiently brings about physical coherence, and all our daily relationships with others provide us with endless opportunities for compassion. Author and philosopher Joseph Campbell said, "When we quit thinking primarily about ourselves and our own preservation, we undergo a truly heroic transformation of consciousness."

Prolonged coherence at a high level (at close to 0.1 Hz) can activate inactive sections of our DNA. Dawson Church in *Healing the Heart of the World* says that thoughts and feelings can turn genes on and off. He says that which genes are activated has to do with our experiences and how we process and react to them. Dr. Rollin McCraty, Dr. Glen Rein, and their team of scientists at the HeartMath Research Center showed that DNA is changed by coherence. Individuals in a test group trained to sustain high coherent emotions were able to change their DNA according to their intentions, even at distances of half a mile from the sample.[2]

Heart feeling is not to be confused with "gut feeling." In the solar plexus area, there is yet another complex brain-like structure of nerve ganglia that is also influenced by emotion. Ideally, the brain, heart and solar plexus should work together and influence each other. In the phenomenon known as entrainment, their rhythms are synchronized, meaning that their electrical patterns form a matching wave-pattern of peaks and troughs. Any kind of stress or negative feelings upsets this delicate balance, but through the many techniques discussed in this book, this balance can be guided back into harmony.

Being centered in positive heart feelings is a quick way to achieve attunement with your Higher Self, with Kuan Yin, or with any other aspect of the Divine. Lower feelings, like worry, greed, lust, sadness, self-pity, blame, etc., create a distorted, chaotic wave-pattern and can produce disease. In *The Intelligent Heart*, David McArthur says, "Love felt deep within the heart is the access code to higher dimensions of energy and intelligence." He describes the large, torus-shaped electromagnetic field of the heart (shaped like a donut) as the receiver and conveyor of this higher intelligence, and says it is at this point where spirit (energy) becomes (enters) matter. It appears to be a transducer for the Source Field.

Mystics and sages have always taught their students to go "into the heart" to pray or meditate. The biblical admonition to "Be Still and Know that I Am God" [Psalm 46:10], is to silence the brain/mind in order to enter our direct connection to the Divine centered in the heart.

The Secret Chamber of The Heart

In *Alchemy of the Heart*, Elizabeth Clare Prophet says, "The heart is the place of great encounters. It's the place where we meet our Real Self and where we meet God." Ancient traditions all speak of a secret place or chamber within the heart. In my own meditations, I was often surprised to find a tropical island there, rather than a room, and sometimes wondered if I was doing something wrong! Recently I was relieved to learn that this island in the heart was written about in ancient Sanskrit texts. The secret place in the heart is experienced differently by different people. It can be a cave, a palace, an island or even perceived as a place of sounds rather than visuals.

Drunvalo Melchizedek's *Living in The Heart* describes several techniques for entering the heart, and the book comes with a practice CD. It is not an intellectual exercise where we merely think of being in the heart—our consciousness actually travels down from the head into the heart. Personally I resisted this practice for years, being averse to going "lower," but now I realize that raising consciousness is not a matter of going higher or lower in location, but higher in vibration. It may be more accurate to say that we access inner realms rather than higher ones. And Divine Love, centered within the heart, is the highest of all vibratory states we can achieve.

We can also access the heart and Kuan Yin quickly using Heartsound, which is created when we do her mantras with love and devotion. Just focus your awareness in your heart, imagine you are breathing through your heart and speaking the mantras through your heart chakra. Some people like to physically bow to the ground with each recitation of the mantra, while others prefer to do so symbolically through the heart, especially if there are time and space constraints.

Keep *feelings* of love, gratitude, joy and appreciation in your heart. Merely thinking about beautiful and lofty, loving thoughts will not do the job. The key to love, healing, abundance, spiritual growth and attunement with the saints and angels is in the nobler heart feelings.

It's also a good idea to keep statues and pictures of Kuan Yin in your environment as she can use them as focuses to send mercy and light into the

50

physical plane. All saints and celestial beings can use their images in this way, as works of art can be accumulators and multipliers of their energy.

1. Institute of HeartMath, see www.HeartMath.com; Rollin McCraty Ph.D. and Glen Rein Ph.D., "Structured Changes in Water and DNA Associated with New Physiologically Measurable States," *Journal of Scientific Explanation*, Vol. 8, No. 3, 1994; pp. 438-439; and Dr. Glen Rein, "Effect of Conscious Intention on Human DNA."

2. Currently ten of our twelve DNA strands are inactivated. Many teachers in the spiritual consciousness movements say we are being prepared for their reactivation in the near future by the planetary acceleration of energy. Increasing compassion and empathy for others is part of that preparation.

CHAPTER 7 ~ **The Physics of Oneness**

Spiritual teacher and researcher Mark Prophet taught that if we call on Kuan Yin throughout the day, she will always respond, whether we ask for personal, community, national or global assistance. She promised through twentieth-century mystics that the giving of her mantras and the pronouncing of her name within the heart makes her immediately one with the physical body of the devotee.

In 1974, the Bodhisattva told a clairaudient devotee that she desires that we develop a "Oneness Consciousness" with others. This is much more than the sense of being all on the same team or part of the same family. We all know how teams and families can squabble and compete with each other.

A real understanding of oneness can be found in the Mayan greeting and goodbye, In *La'kesh*, which means "You are another me." Some people have had the experience of actually seeing their own face on everyone they encounter and simultaneously feeling the underlying unity of everything. This is not a mere intellectual understanding but a profound, direct experience that produces a great delight in the heart. It can last for several minutes to several hours or days. In a few rare cases it lasts for months.

Yet God is not many gods. He is still the All One. How can this be? *In Science of the Spoken Word*, Mark Prophet says, "It is the nature of the Infinite One to multiply His Being infinitely and still remain one. (One-times-one-times-one *ad infinitum* always equals one.) Thus God the Father and God the Son may be actualized in man and woman over and over again and still remain inviolate as the Divine One." The One individuates itself in each of us, but this does not create separation— on the contrary, the potential is there for total union with the One.

Many writers, teachers and spiritual leaders of different paths have observed that a great evolutionary shift is now occurring on the planet as people from all walks of life are awakening from their illusion of separateness. As the Infinite One multiplies itself infinitely as man, woman, child, angel, archangel, cosmic being and so on ever higher, consciousness is singular, not plural, and we all share in it. Spiritual beings of higher dimensions exist at higher frequencies of this consciousness, while beings existing in lower dimensions are lesser evolved facets of the One. The seeming separation between beings in different dimensions is one of frequency, not location.

Thus one of my teachers said that Kuan Yin asked us to see all others as "another me," another aspect of the One, and therefore to treat others as ourselves. There is no longer any "me versus you" duality. (See our final chapter on a Hawaiian ritual that expresses this perfectly.)

Author and teacher Eckhart Tolle says the transformation of this area of human consciousness is no longer a luxury but has become a necessity. He says, "Your Innermost Self, of who you are, is inseparable from stillness. This is the I Am that is deeper than name and form."

As John Maxwell Taylor explains in *The Power of I Am*, a quick way to lose your sense of separation is to get out of your head. You can do this by sending your awareness into your legs, arms and torso, keeping your attention centered in the heart, yet also simultaneously dispersed throughout your entire body. You basically disassociate from your outer mind. With a bit of practice, this rewards you with a rapid connection to the divine observer within, a sense of oneness with your surroundings and a loss of personal ego identification. It takes more practice to sustain this for longer and longer time periods, but eventually with perseverance, you will be able to maintain this state through all your daily activities. The key is to stay out of the thought-based awareness in your head and remain in heart-based, wordless awareness. The added bonus is that this pleasurable experience keeps you serene and unruffled.

Some Astounding Physics

Let's look at how some of the tenets of quantum mechanics support these ideas. (I could write a whole book on this, but other authors have already done so, and are listed in the Bibliography.) One of the basic concepts is that of non-locality as demonstrated by Bell's Theorem. This shows that subatomic particles can affect each other:

• Over any distance in the universe

• Instantaneously (faster than the speed of light)

• Without diminishing

• Without crossing the intervening space

• Without an energy source or expenditure

In short, the essence of non-locality is immediate, direct, unmitigated contact.

The second concept is that of phase entanglement, meaning once connected, always connected. Subatomic "particles" exchange some of their wave phase information, which leads to permanent connection and the ability to exchange information forever. How entangled is everything? It has been said that each glass of water we drink contains one molecule of hemlock poison taken by Socrates. And if we go all the way back, everything was connected before the Big Bang. The atoms of our bodies have been around since the dawn of creation.

The third concept is that "matter" doesn't exist. Yes, you read that right! Matter is not solid as we perceive it to be. Those little spheres in diagrams of atoms are not material. They are compressed packs of energy; and energy is not matter. The appearance of mass is caused by the wave centers of standing waves. The human brain is a wave frequency analyzer and interprets these as form and mass. All matter is connected to all other matter by its waves. (So now we can appreciate how prayers and mantras work at a distance.) The universe is considered by physicists (and mystics) to be a vast field of energy, and that subquantum, electromagnetic fluctuations fill every part of cosmos. This is the Zero Point energy field, which Russian experiments now demonstrate originates from the non-electromagnetic Source Field that appears to have gravitational and spin energy.

The fourth concept is that of the observer effect, which states that observation changes outcome. When observed, electrons tend to behave like particles; when not being observed, they behave like probability waves. The results of quantum experiments depend on whether or not someone is looking! (This again sheds light on the intent and visualization factors of our prayer work. Are we really there, actively engaged in our manifestations, or are we reciting by rote, hardly paying attention, barely even observing?)

These concepts drove scientists nuts until they decided to factor in conscious observation and intention, which is our fifth concept. Research shows that consciousness changes the outcome of experiments. Consciousness cannot be removed from the equation, because everything that we are aware of exists in the field of our consciousness. Scientist Dean Radin, director of the Consciousness Research Laboratory at the University of Nevada, writes that consciousness:

• Extends beyond the individual

• Has quantum-field-like properties

• Affects outcomes of events

• Affects inanimate objects

• Is non-local in nature

Science is now catching on to the idea that we are individuated aspects of the one consciousness of the universe, which is divine spirit. How do electrons always know when they are being observed? Their energy is the energy of consciousness—they are not separate from it.

Physicists say that all living beings are coalescences of energy and consciousness within an infinite field of electromagnetic energy and that we are connected to everything in cosmos. The energy of consciousness (which includes magnetism) is now considered to be the primary reality and the basic fabric of the universe. Our individual frequencies form an interference pattern (overlapping waves) with every other conscious being in cosmos.

Some scientists consider the universe to be holographic. The nature of a hologram (which is an interference pattern) is that the entire hologram is within every part, but on a smaller scale. For example, in the holographic image of a tree, the entire image of the tree will be found in any and every piece of the image, no matter how small.

The implication of this is that when you change yourself and your world through the recitation of Kuan Yin mantras or with any sincere spiritual practice, you affect every part of the universe by changing your portion of the cosmic hologram. Every single electron is connected with every other electron in the field.

Once we understand this, we may no longer think that we can do as we please in private because "it doesn't hurt anyone else." There's no such thing as an isolated thought, feeling or action. This should be reason enough to clean up the media and the arts. The vibrations of shock, anger, fear, sadness, etc., of so much of its content affects everyone and all of cosmos on some level. That's why it would be advisable, in order to maintain the harmony and integrity of one's forcefield, to limit television and movie viewing to documentaries and content that is clean, uplifting and nonviolent.

Author Lynne McTaggart, who compiles research in quantum science, notes that the experiments of Backster, Popp and Korotkov suggest that "Every last thought appeared to augment or diminish something else's light." In *The Field*, she reports that "All living beings are a coalescence of energy in a field of energy connected to every other thing in the world. This pulsating energy field is the central engine of our being and our consciousness."

Nobel Prize-winning physicist Erwin Schrodinger said, "Mind, by its very nature, is a singular entity. I should say the overall number of minds is just one."

CHAPTER 8 ~ **Dissolving Karma with the Flame of Grace**

by Christine Meiner

The Law of Karma is the law of cause and effect and is reflected in the biblical admonition, "That which you sow, so shall you also reap" [Galatians 6:7] and the more colloquial saying, "What goes around comes around!" We have been given free will to create our worlds by making use of the light-energy that flows continuously into our hearts and from there throughout our bodies. This energy is shaped and molded by our every thought, word and action.

As we learn from quantum physics, everything is energy encoded with information. Every erg of electronic-light energy that we use in the arenas of thought, word and deed is imprinted with our individual identifying mark. In essence, this makes us accountable for all the misuses of the light that has ever flowed through our consciousness, being and world. All energy used in a positive, harmonious fashion is stored up in our "treasures in heaven," but any that we have released in a negative form is "enslaved" with this imprint unless and until it is freed and "washed clean" through the application of a higher vibration—enter the Flame of Grace.

Thought & Feeling

All electronic light flowing through us responds to our thoughts and feelings. It moves out in a circle and by the Law of Attraction returns to us with more energy of its kind. In this way, we experience the multiplied results of what we have created with the energy at our command. Thought sets the intention of creation. It is masculine (yang in nature) and is the mold into which feeling (the feminine aspect, yin in nature) is poured. It has been said that thoughts will determine the *number of electrons* in an atomic structure and feelings will determine its *oscillation rate.*

In the physical world, both thought and feeling are required for physical manifestation and together they will determine the nature and quality of that creation. The atoms of our bodies tend to respond more readily to our thoughts and feelings because our bodies vibrate at a higher frequency than most other matter, and because our bodies are connected to our spiritual heart, the inner distribution point of that light energy.

It is becoming increasingly important that each of us gains control over our creative faculties. As the frequency of our whole planet rises, the physical manifestations of our thoughts and feelings are also accelerating. By developing conscious control over what occupies our thoughts and feelings, we have the opportunity to master our life circumstances at a higher degree. Indeed, some say this is the main reason why we are here in earth's schoolroom. Meditation and chanting the mantras in this book will help to quiet your mind and open your heart to inner listening. A key to self-mastery is to remain centered in and connected to the Source of all Life.

While we are still learning to master our thoughts and feelings, we may often create situations that are not to our liking. Just like a potter learning to shape the clay, perfection requires practice. During this time of experimentation, we have the free-will opportunity to choose how we want to respond to our learning experiences in this world—to react to or forgive ourselves and others.

The Violet Flame of Grace

Purple Chalcedony

During prayer and meditation, many spiritual devotees with their inner sight have seen themselves surrounded by an intense light of a magenta, purple or violet hue. Violet light, having the highest vibratory rate in the visible color spectrum, has some unique qualities. It can increase the oscillation of electrons and even complex molecular structures. It is thereby able to raise the frequency of matter and consciousness, including the memory and record of our past creations. This is reminiscent of the scripture, "Though your sins be like scarlet, I will make them as white as snow." [Isaiah 1:18] Applying the violet fire can transmute returning negative karma that vibrates at a lower frequency before it outpictures on the physical plane.

58

If you wish to employ additional aid from among the gifts of Mother Earth, the action of the violet light can be magnified by Purple Chalcedony, Sugilite, and Amethyst crystals. Its high frequency can be stored and transmitted from within their molecular structures. The violet frequencies are increased on Saturdays, and the musical note B-sharp translates these frequencies into sound. The Chinese and Sanskrit seed syllables and mantras in this book have been encoded by Kuan Yin to emit the violet frequencies as well. Visualizing all the shades of the pink/violet spectrum, with its many hues ranging from orchid and magenta to indigo-blue purple while invoking violet fire can widen these applications.

Mark Prophet taught that invocation of this Flame of Grace could be directed by conscious focus into any undesirable situation or world condition. He said that through visualization, prayer and mantra, we can send transmuting energies, mercy and compassion to any person or situation.

Kuan Yin has chosen to master this violet frequency in order to assist those who desire to undo their past karmas and negative creations. Many of her depictions show her outpouring a vial of this elixir to her supplicants and to the world at large. Because she extends this Flame of Grace to all life, we revere her as the Goddess of Mercy and Compassion. By applying our thoughts, feelings, words and visualizations along with loving-kindness to generate light, we choose to be divine instruments, partners with Kuan Yin, extending mercy and compassion to all life.

Invoking Violet Light

How do we invoke this violet light? Along with the giving of any of Kuan Yin's mantras, there are several specific violet-fire invocations included in a later chapter. Kuan Yin's vast momentum of compassion and forgiveness magnifies and multiplies our invocations, making our work more effective for changing our personal conditions and the greater world around us.

By visualizing while invoking the violet fire, our feelings are engaged along with our thoughts, and the light substance is more easily condensed and made physical. Heartsound has been defined as the joint use of heart, mind and sound in this work. Before beginning our prayers and mantras, we can ask for the transmutation of the cause, effect, record and memory of all our karmic debt, and we can maximize our calls to include all on earth who are similarly afflicted.

CHAPTER 9 ~ **The Violet Light as Universal Purifier**

Some spiritual schools like The Summit Lighthouse teach that every color ray has a divine quality, and that Kuan Yin mantras vibrate with the color violet. Her color is magenta, which is part of the violet group that includes lavender, purple, pink and orchid. They also teach that violet is the color frequency of mercy, forgiveness, freedom and transmutation, which is a positive change into something higher. There are different mantras for each color of the rainbow, as well as some of the pastel colors like peach and aqua, and the mantras' sounds have a matching frequency pattern with their corresponding color and virtue. Some clairvoyants can see the colors of sound and some clairaudients can hear the sound of color! Their extrasensory perceptions are expanded to see and hear a wider bandwidth of photon (light) and phonon (sonic) wavelengths than the rest of us.

The most useful color application for all situations is violet, as its frequencies are cleansing, healing and transformative. It was predicted by Saint Germain in the 1930s that in the future we will clean our homes with violet light. It will also be used to clean up pollution when enough people give violet-light mantras consistently. This can be as simple as saying, "O violet light, come cleanse and heal me and all the earth now!"

It's interesting to note that ultraviolet light, the highest frequency on the spectrum, is used to purify water. Additionally, Washington State University researchers found that UV light impacts gene repair. Their study also showed it activated the creation of defense proteins. Although UV light is not what I'm referring to directly in this chapter, rather its energetic counterpart, these examples show what can be achieved with invisible light rays.

In the last century, teachers like the Ballards, the Prophets and others taught that the violet ray, also known as the 7th ray because of its position in the spectrum, is much more than a physical light. It is an energy of the Holy Spirit that appears as violet to clairvoyants. Since ancient times, this was a secret knowledge given only to the highest saints and adepts of East and West. Of the spiritual frequencies, violet is the closest vibratory match to the physical color violet, which vibrates at 731 trillion times a second, having the greatest ability to penetrate matter at atomic levels. Dannion Brinkley who survived three near-death experiences saw it on the other side and said, "The violet flame is a light that serves all spiritual heritages."

Saint Germain

The use of violet light, often referred to as violet flame or fire, was first revealed to the general public in the 1930s by the master Saint Germain who delivered the teachings through Guy Ballard (pen-named Godfre Ray King). This story is documented in his still popular books, *Unveiled Mysteries* and *The I Am Discourses*.

In the last embodiment before his ascension, Saint Germain was known throughout Europe as *Le Comte de Saint Germain*, a nobleman with miraculous powers. His story is told in the documentary, "The Man Who Would Not Die" that aired as part of the "In Search Of" television series.

Mark Prophet, another one of Saint Germain's messengers, noted that before Saint Germain was granted permission by earth's spiritual overseers to release the knowledge of the violet fire, the only ways to erase past karmic debt to life were through the slow and laborious methods of suffering, self-denial, service to others, or lifetimes of prayer. Although these methods are still valid and required to balance part of our energy accounts, the majority of this work can now be done with the use of 7th-ray visualizations and mantras, thus shortening the time for final liberation from rebirth on this planet.

Dawn Covington, Ed.D., one of the foremost authorities on Saint Germain and the violet ray, teaches that Saint Germain gained this dispensation on behalf of all people of all faiths for the consuming of their negative energies and for the saving of the earth. He declared that simply attaining enlightenment or God-realization is not our ticket to liberation from this planet, because we still have to clean up our misused energies, balance our debts to life, and fulfill our earthly divine plan before we can move on.

The consensus of my teachers is that to take the best advantage of this dispensation and to win our victory, those who learn of the violet light in their youth should dedicate at least fifteen minutes a day to the giving of the mantras. The older we are when we start, the more we need to do on a daily basis. For those of us over age 50, a half hour a day is better, as generally speaking, we probably have less time left than younger people. Some people do an hour or more daily, especially on weekends. Others who are employed in physical rather than mental occupations find they can do their memorized prayers and mantras while they work.

One truck driver I know has violet-fire decrees recorded on CDs and tapes with which he chants ten-to-twelve hours a day as he drives. Many of my friends also recite the mantras whenever they are driving and while doing yoga. It's good to do these while watching the news and projecting its rays of light into situations on the screen and for the mitigation of world karma. Invoking the overshadowing presence of Kuan Yin, Saint Germain and the violet-fire angels can multiply the power of your work.

Thousands of people testify to the miracles that 7th-ray mantras have produced in their lives when used consistently with faith and love. Many call it the fountain of youth, as daily use of the violet light slows down the aging process.

Amethyst

There are many testimonials of bodily, financial, relationship, community and world change—all accomplished by the application of the spiritual energies invoked by violet-fire prayers, affirmations and mantras, including the Kuan Yin mantras. These Heartsound frequencies are an effective tool for transforming negative thoughts and feelings, as many users have noted.

The violet light has been referred to as the "miracle transmuting flame" and the "cosmic eraser" because its frequency and vibration removes negativity, including negative records held around the electrons of anything it is directed into.

According to Dr. Covington who teaches *The Pure Joy System* of employing the violet light, Saint Germain said the violet fire consumes the negative energy residing in our subconscious that produces the unwanted conditions in our lives. It erases our negative energy records bit-by-bit, which is the key to permanent liberation from the physical plane. She also teaches that violet is composed of two colors, blue and ruby. The magnetic wave-pattern of ruby demagnetizes the negative records held by electrons. The blue frequency wave repolarizes them to their original blueprint and purity. According to quan-tum mechanics, waves have infinite capacity for information exchange and storage.

How do you access this higher dimensional violet light? Besides reciting the Kuan Yin mantras, it can also be done with affirmations and visualization, by playing waltzes with their 3/4 time rhythm and by having the various hues of the violet family in your surroundings and clothing. Amethyst crystals, Sugilite stones and the scent of lavender also carry its vibration. All of these can be agents of transformation by focusing violet wavelengths around you. Perhaps it would be more accurate to say that higher beings, saints and angels can focus the violet fire frequencies using these vehicles.

Since the violet frequency cancels out wave overlays holding negative records, many people keep the music of Strauss waltzes playing continuously in their homes. Waltzes are also good for the heart as they are aligned with its natural rhythm. The 3/4 time waltzes helped to raise the consciousness of Europeans in the 19th century. By contrast, it has been proven that the syncopated 4/4 time of most Western music (rock, jazz, blues, pop, rap, etc.) with its typical non-symmetrical emphasis on the 3rd beat rather than the downbeat, throws off our natural rhythms and should be avoided.

More people like teachers, yoga instructors, store owners and people in the healing arts like dentists, chiropractors and holistic therapists are now finding creative ways to access the violet light in their professions. Besides doing the visualizations and mantras themselves, they may paint walls a pale lavender or periwinkle, use purple themed decor and advertising, play waltz music in the background, set out large Amethyst crystals, and display pictures or antique statues of Kuan Yin. Where appropriate, they may also teach clients to use violet-fire visualizations and affirmations.

Visualizing Violet

For visualization, you can picture the violet group of colors either individually or in any combination. Many people visualize flames in these colors around and through whatever person, place or condition to which their mantras are dedicated. Some people like to use images of violet fireworks, some visualize violet baths, and others think of it as a purple or magenta liquid light being poured out into places and situations, or as a purple rain.

Visualization is important because it converts our intent into a frequency overlay on the sound vibrations of our prayers, affirmation and mantras. Japanese researcher Masaru Emoto photographed the results of the power of frequency and intent as it affects the crystalline structure of water. These can be viewed in his *Messages from Water* series of books. Polluted water formed distorted crystals, as did water with negative words or phrases taped to the jar. After polluted water was prayed over, the crystals formed were beautiful, as were the crystals from water with positive words taped to the container. The same was true for water exposed to music. Harmonious, classical music created lovely symmetrical crystals while the jagged rhythms of rock, jazz and pop music created disorganized crystals. This has profound implications when we consider that our bodies are about 70% water and that our food and drink are bombarded by the frequencies of music with discordant rhythms in stores.

Because a number of people have had the direct experience of the heart being both a portal and convergence point for higher energies, some spiritual aspirants focus their concentration on violet light streaming forth through their hearts, or from the heart of Kuan Yin or Saint Germain, and into the condition they are working on.

You can picture your body, family, pets, home, car, town, state, country or planet bathed in various hues of violet as you recite. Every personal, national and planetary problem could be solved if people would rally to the use of the violet light. Clairvoyants see a lot of violet in the auras of people who do the Kuan Yin or violet-ray mantras. You will find some of these mantras and decrees in Part III of this book.

Crystals

Sugilite

Many people place Sugilite and large Amethyst crystals in the area where they pray or meditate, and it is not just because of the color that they are used as a focus for violet fire. Amethyst is a type of quartz crystal. All quartz can receive and transmit electromagnetic frequencies. People who have done a lot of spiritual work with crystals are convinced that crystals are "alive" and have some type of consciousness. Whereas life as we usually think of it is carbon-based, crystals are silicon-based. (Sugilite is a complex silicate.) Scientists have found that silicon has the same principles of life as carbon. Oceanic silicon life-forms have been discovered that are conscious and that reproduce. Nicola Tesla, probably the greatest scientific genius the world has seen, said, "In a crystal we have the clear evidence of a formative life principal, and though we cannot understand the life of a crystal, it is nonetheless a living being."

Crystal authority Robert Simmons, author of *Stones of the New Consciousness*, states, "Sugilite is perhaps the most powerful stone for calling in the violet fire of purification. This energy can be of immeasurable benefit for those on the spiritual path, for it tends to burn away the "gray spots" in the auric field, removing negative attachments and karmic influences. Sugilite's violet-fire energy makes it impossible for parasitic entities from the astral plane to remain in one's auric field. When one begins to wear or carry Sugilite, an energetic cleansing process is initiated."

Crystals are used for receiving electromagnetic signals in radios and computers and human thought is also an electromagnetic frequency. Quartz is used in all high-tech communication devices, and the ancients regarded it as a device for communicating between worlds. The ability of quartz to transduce mechanical energy into electromagnetic energy is known as the piezo-electric effect. Some consider natural quartz, especially raw, piezo-electric quartz crystal, as having the capacity to interact with human consciousness even across time and space.

Researcher Marc Vogel, a former scientist at IBM, concluded that "crystal emits a vibration which extends and amplifies the powers of the user's mind. Like a laser, it radiates energy in a coherent, highly concentrated form, and this energy may be transmitted to objects and people at will." Vogel developed a way of cutting quartz crystals that greatly amplifies their healing power.

Crystals like Amethyst are mostly silicon dioxide. The earth is also largely composed of silicon dioxide, so because of morphic resonance, whatever we project into a crystal (like violet light via meditation and the sonic waves of the spoken word) will resonate with similar crystalline structures of the entire planet. According to Rupert Sheldrake's theory of morphic resonance, everything of similar structural frequencies will resonate together, whether in physical contact or not. Crystals taken out of the earth are still connected with the earth by their common morphic field.

Tools like crystals can help and enhance our spiritual journey, but it all must start in the heart, and in our own connection to the Divine. Again, Omraam says it well:

Quartz crystals

"Small though they are, precious stones are particles of matter capable of holding cosmic power. But you shouldn't rely on them and believe they will protect you, heal you and give you powers; if you don't do any work, they will be useless. A stone is a sort of aerial, and like an aerial it needs a function, messages to transmit. Around the stone, there are forces moving and vibrating, but it is up to you to focus them, to give them direction. Each precious stone has already been prepared by nature to pick up certain energies from the cosmos and broadcast and propagate them. But just possessing a precious stone is not enough if you wish to benefit from its properties; you have to learn to use it to do your own inner work."

[Omraam Mikhaël Aïvanhov, Daily Meditations at www.Prosveta.org]

CHAPTER 10 ~ **The Secrets of Sound,**
Sonic Healing & Mantras

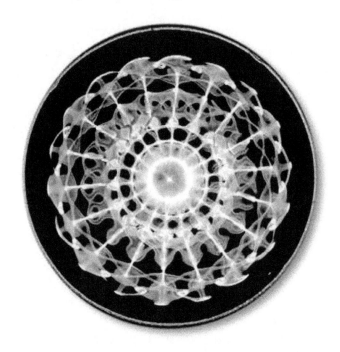

This elaborate 18-faceted jewel is actually a snapshot of a dynamic process of circulation generated when audible sound frequencies were projected into a shallow Petri dish filled with water. Light reflecting off the surface of the water highlights the standing waves which arose as a result of the resonance.

Like all mantras and affirmations, the Kuan Yin mantras are normally spoken aloud because, according to esoteric tradition, sound is one of the key ingredients of creation and transformation. The mantras can be done silently where necessary, like in public places or at your workplace, but some sound is always better, even a whisper.

The various ancient religions both East and West concur that creation in the material realm began with sound. Both Hindu and Christian scriptures state, "In the beginning was the Word," which is sound or vibration. Many traditions also speak of a transcendental primordial sound that created and sustains the universe, and advanced meditators connect with a direct experience of this "soundless sound." Two ancient texts from India, the *Laksmi Tantra* and the *Shiva Sutra*, describe the universe as being composed of fifty basic vibrations divided into three categories: audible sound, subtle sound and silent sound.

Russian researchers have found that our genetic code follows the rules of human language, and that our languages reflect our DNA. Russian biophysicist Pjotr Garajev and his team modulated sound frequency patterns onto a laser, and used this to alter DNA frequencies and thereby genetic information. It was demonstrated in experiments that living DNA is influenced by language-modulated laser rays. This shows why affirmations can affect us physically, because DNA naturally responds to language.

Russian experimenters have transmitted the genetic information from salamander embryos onto frog embryos simply by applying sound frequencies and language. The frog embryos grew into salamanders and reproduced as such. They demonstrated what "new-thought" teachers have known for decades, that our bodies can be programmed by thought and language.

A vibration (sound) of a sustained frequency (pitch) is a tone, and the ancients recognized the relationship between physical form and tone. The giant statues of Memnon released a tone when struck by sunlight at dawn. Some postulate that the pyramids and other enormous stone structures were set in place using inaudible sonic vibrations to activate antigravity.

Sages and philosophers spoke of the "music of the spheres" and it is known that planets emit infrasonic sound of such low frequencies that it is measured in cycles per year. A few years ago, scientists recorded a continuous subsonic hum emanating from the earth. NASA's Voyager I and II space probes recorded deep space "music."

In *The World Is Sound—Nada Brahma* by Joachim-Ernst Berendt, astronomers Robert M. Sickels and Jeff Lightman describe these sounds from their radio astronomy: "The giant planet Jupiter produces its own peculiar noise—huge rapid sighs like the intense roaring of a distant surge... The sun makes noises too, hisses and crackling in quietude, and roars of alarming intensity."

We normally experience sound as a pressure wave, yet it has an electromagnetic component when it is encoded on radio waves. Crystal radios receiving electromagnetic radio signals, transduce them back into sound waves. The human ear converts sound-wave motion to electrical impulses. In 1989 experiments, modulated sound was combined with a microwave carrier, then sound was induced into the subject's brain by radiating it with bursts of microwaves in a special wave format. Inaudible sound can also travel as thought waves and be deciphered by consciousness, like when we pick up on a friend's thoughts. It has been postulated that the crop circles in England are sometimes created sonically as high-pitched trilling sounds can be heard immediately before their formation and end as soon as the crop is flattened.

Our observable world is a world of form and many experiments have shown that form is related to and sustained by sound. Sound frequencies can bring manifestation into the material realm when coupled with focused attention and feeling.

In his book, *Cymatics*, Swiss physician and scientist Hans Jenny shows how he created various forms in substances like powders, pastes, metal filings and liquids just by using different sounds. As some become spirals, some flower shaped and so on, he definitely demonstrated that the world of form can be changed and shaped by sound and that dissonant sounds create chaotic shapes. Alexander Lauterwasser did similar work in Germany.

Hans Jenny found that increased frequencies lead to more complex designs, and increased amplitudes could lead to eruptions. His experiments also showed that intoning the vowel sounds of ancient Hebrew and Sanskrit caused vibrating sand to form their written symbols—evidence that these ancient languages are based on what we call today the optical manifestation of a sonic interference pattern. Since then, further research by others show that sound can form and rearrange molecules.

In his Internet article, "Cymatics: The Science of the Future?", German investigator Peter Petersson discusses the research in this field. (Cymatics is the study of how vibrations generate and influence form.) He reviews the work of 18th century musician and physicist Ernst Chladni who pioneered ways to make sound waves create visible forms when he drew his violin bow across the edge of sand-covered plates. Through this and other means, he created patterns now called Chladni Figures [see illustration]. He showed that sound affects physical matter and creates geometric forms.

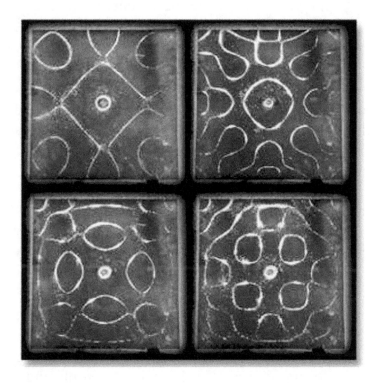

A thin metal sheet, fixed in the center, is excited in vibrational modes with a large loudspeaker. Fine sand sprinkled on the plate shows various modes of vibration in a plane.

Traditions from all cultures have long stated that sound (which is vibration) creates matter. Quantum theory now supports this with observations that waves collapse into "particles." The basic nature of everything in the universe is wave vibration. All vibration has sound, but only a tiny band of frequencies are audible to the human ear.

In *The Ancient Secret of the Flower of Life*, Drunvalo Melchizedek says that "dimensional levels are nothing but base-rate wavelengths," and that Bell Laboratories discovered that our three-dimensional, physical universe has a basic wavelength of 7.23 cm. He noted that in a spiritual sense this 7.23 cm wavelength is "Om," the sound of the universe. As the Bible states, "Without the Word was not anything made that was made" [John 1:3].

A type of sound vibration is the basic energy source from which the universe came into being. All matter is merely vibrating energy that emits sound. The slower and lower the frequency, the greater the density of the form. Solidity is an illusion. Some scientists think that the Big Bang was an extremely low note way below the threshold of vibrations perceptible to the human ear, and this energy emission is still expanding outward as time/space. When a recording of the OM is played through a resonator plate, the sand on top vibrates into the Sri Yantra pattern, the pattern of creation, a complex mandala of triangles inside a circle [see illustration below].

Sound can also be used destructively. Several decades ago, German scientists supposedly developed a weapon capable of shattering a four-inch-thick metal plate at a range of two miles using low-frequency sound waves. Angels and masters, through their communications to spiritual intuitives, have warned that the misuse of sound, especially in the many types of discordant music popular today, can cause the destruction of the soul and the sinking of continents, as happened in prerecorded history when earlier civilizations were destroyed using similar sound technologies. This is not so far-fetched when we remember that, like everything else in the universe, souls and continents alike are simply wave-fields encoded with information.

Sri Yantra

72

Sonic Healing

In the past half century, the healing ability of music and sound has been the subject of much research. Every atom, molecule, cell and organ has a vibrational frequency, and if any of these are "off," imbalances of disease can occur in the body and mind. In England, Dr. Peter Guy Manners pioneered healing treatments using harmonic frequencies to restore the natural and correct resonance of the body, thereby restoring health.

Most sounds found in nature also have a healing effect. Interestingly, it has been found that the frequencies orthopedists use to strengthen bones and knit fractures are the same as a cat's purr! Some hospitals now have a harpist playing in the operating room, while others use recorded harp music. The harmonics of harp strings have a proven, powerful, calming effect on the nervous system, reducing blood pressure and normalizing irregular heartbeats.

Many experiments show that the best instrument for sonic healing is the human voice. Gregorian chants, for example, have a positive effect on the central nervous system and brain. Studies at Duke University show that daily prayer can reduce the stress hormone cortisol by 22% and much more if done aloud. Research at Germany's Witten/Herdecke University found that women who prayed aloud for only five minutes a day were 81% more relaxed than women who didn't.

It's been observed that when we sound a tone, like the sustained pitch of an Om, for example, it is a source of healing for our body. With the aid of a camera on a microscope, French bioenergeticist Fabien Maman studied the effects of sounds and music on cells. When he looked at cancer cells, the most remarkable results occurred when he sang musical scales into them. He noted, "The structure disorganized extremely quickly. The human voice carries something in its vibration that makes it more powerful than any musical instrument: consciousness. The cancer cells could not support the progressive accumulation of vibratory frequencies. As soon as I introduced a third frequency in the sequence, the cells began to destabilize." A couple of musical instruments with a lot of overtones also made the cancer cells disintegrate and ultimately explode. In Maman's *The Role of Music in the Twenty-First Century* he writes, "The vibration of sound plays a determinant role in the transformation of cellular structure. As long as we played the whole chromatic musical scale for the same length of time, the diseased cell was too disrupted to stabilize."

Music and sound have a particularly strong effect on the emotions. Sustained toning of vowels or elongating single syllables like the *bija* (seed essence or seed syllable) mantras can change the vibratory rate of cells and organs. It can release energy blocks and resolve records of trauma held in the body. Numerous books have been written on this subject and are readily available via the Internet. (See Recommended Reading.)

A *Bija Mantra* consists of a single, powerful syllable that does not have meaning as a word, but becomes an energetic experience through much repetition. The tone can be directed and focused into any area of the body that needs help. The different bijas activate different energy frequencies, for example:

- **Shrim** (*Shreem*)—abundance

- **Dum** (*Doom*)—protection

- **Gum** (*Gahm)*—obstacle removal

- **Hrim** (*Hreem*)—clarity

- **Eim** (*I'm*)—knowledge

Many different vocalizations can be used for healing when encoded with intention. We can intone the Om, which is the primary bija mantra and the intonation of the name of God, the source of all existence. OM is also said to be the sound emanating from the sun and the stars throughout cosmos. You can recite Kuan Yin's mantra, *Om Mani Padme Hum*, or simpy her bija mantra "hrih." The syllables "hu" and "ah" also have a long history of use for energy balancing and are very good for the heart as well as other organs. The *Our Father* and *Hail Mary* are considered to be mantras in the Christian tradition.

When using Kuan Yin mantras, whether for personal or planetary conditions, it is important to encode your intentions on the sound, and this is done with visualization and feeling. In his excellent book, *Sound Medicine*, Wayne Perry says that sound is a "carrier wave for consciousness," and advises guarding our consciousness from the pollution of unhealthy words and sounds as they have a "deleterious effect on our hearts and minds." He particularly refers to profanity as one example.

Perry also writes that "because of its all-pervading capacity to serve as a multidimensional vehicle for information, love is the most potent of all healing vibrations...that can influence all other frequencies to shift to wholeness and healing."

The Power of Mantra

Ancient Hindus and Buddhists used the power of sound in mantras to achieve enlightenment and union with the Divine. Kuan Yin's mantras were repeated aloud to break up negative energy patterns. Shanti Hee, who wrote Chapter 18 for this book, says that toning vowels and short mantras in the heart during meditation is a method of entering Zero Point that works consistently once it is mastered through practice. She uses this method for healing earth energies and communing with Kuan Yin.

Since ancient times in the Himalayas, those who knew how to correctly use mantras possessed power to create and control forces. What is expressed by sound in mantra does come into manifestation according to the cosmic law of cycles, but this work cannot be done solely in a mechanical way; otherwise, recordings or prayer wheels could do the manifesting for us. It is the divine power residing in the heart and activated through Heartsound that does the work.

In *Healing Mudras*, Sabrina Mesko writes that mantras "have a powerful effect on your entire being when chanted repeatedly during meditation or mudra practice. The hard palate in your mouth has fifty-eight energy points that connect to your entire body. Stimulating these points with sound vibrations affects your mental and physical energy. Certain sounds that stimulate these points have a very healing quality. When you repeat aloud or whisper these ancient mantras or scientific healing-sound combinations, the meridians on your hard palate are activated in a specific order that repatterns the energy of your system."

Mantra syllables have no intrinsic power on their own, but they can focus the frequencies of already existing forces. Their full effectiveness also depends on the use of visualization, feeling, intent, rhythm, steadfastness of concentration and heart connection. It is especially helpful to connect with the spiritual being who originally sponsored and empowered the mantra.

Thus you can see that mantras are not a magical easy road, but require physical, mental, emotional and spiritual exertion, along with consistent effort toward self-improvement.

Mantras additionally have a spiritual frequency that is beyond the vibration of audible, physical sound waves. The power of this spiritual aspect depends on the devotion, attitude and purity of heart of the individual. If one recites from the heart as well as the throat, creating Heartsound, the inner sound connects with higher beings and the spiritual universe. Obtaining the spiritual effects also requires sincere belief, a willingness to renounce our bad habits and continual effort toward our spiritual evolution.

It has been noted by saints and sages of both east and west that "the call compels the answer," so Kuan Yin will always assist us with fulfilling our needs provided we daily make a sincere request for her aid.

CHAPTER 11 ~ **Visualization & Feeling to Enhance Manifestation**

In my workshops on the life-changing power of affirmations, I always include a segment on visualization and feeling because these are prime ingredients of the creation formula. Any manifestation recipe must contain these two ingredients to achieve the best results.

We are all connected at the level of the unconscious mind, which understands and responds more powerfully to images and feelings than to words. Jonathan Goldman says, "Vocalization plus visualization equals manifestation." Remember that waves have unlimited capacity for information storage. Sound can also be encoded with positive heart feelings to become Heartsound.

The first key to success with visualization is detail. We can use humorous details, tiny details, unusual details or whatever we wish, but it must be as vivid and specific as possible for our desired outcome. The second key to success is repetition. Repetition not only opens the door to the subconscious—just ask any advertising agency and the news media—it also creates new beliefs and neural pathways in the brain and body.

Rewiring the Brain

In a NASA experiment, astronauts were equipped with goggles that made them see everything upside down. They had to wear these goggles twenty-four hours a day. In the beginning, they were extremely disoriented and stressed. On the twenty-sixth day of the experiment, one of the astronauts began seeing the world right-side up again while wearing the goggles. During the next few days, the same thing happened to the other astronauts.

This means it took about thirty days on average to rewire their brains. Further experiments showed this would not happen if the goggles were removed before this time period had elapsed, even if they were only removed for a little while.

Applying this to ourselves, it means we cannot skip a day here and there when working for specific changes in ourselves or our lives. Skipping a day collapses the foundation and we must begin again. When doing a mantra for forty days, or however many days we have chosen, they must be consecutive, and with the appropriate images and feelings to create the necessary connections both in the brain and the collective unconscious.

My Kuan Yin Statue

A few years ago, I saw a large Chinese antique statue of Kuan Yin for sale, and wanted to buy it for my bedroom. Once a week I went to visit the statue, then every day for the rest of the week I'd visualize it in my room. Each time I went back to where it was for sale, I memorized more details to use for my daily imaging at home. I would also pick it up to create a better sense memory of its size and weight, then I mentally put it in my car and drove it home. After about a month of this, I received an extra check that was almost the price of the statue. The statue now sits in front of me as I write this book.

Never underestimate the power of detail and of repetition. The brain cannot tell the difference between a real experience and a vividly imaged one because the neurons fire just the same. Goals and new beliefs are also more easily planted into the subconscious mind when we have a slow theta brainwave pattern of 4 to 7 cycles per second, which is natural immediately before the onset of sleep. There are recordings available that put you into this theta state, or you can get there by closing your eyelids and rolling back your eyes as if trying to look out through the top of your head. Keep the eyes in this position and do silent affirmations and visualization, as speaking aloud could bring back the faster beta brainwave pattern. Holding this eye position is not comfortable because our muscles are not used to it.

It's important to keep your goals positive and loving, for when your consciousness is changed, so is the entire field of consciousness because it exists in the quantum, non-local domain where the concept of separation has no meaning. Thoughts send out measurable waves—they don't just stay in your head.

Also visualize the colors of the violet group, especially the pink/violet or magenta, which is Kuan Yin's color. Visualize these colors as you feel guided to, moving through and around yourself, your home, and other people, places and conditions.

The Power of Feelings

Kuan Yin mantras are traditionally done with feelings of love directed to Kuan Yin, other people, the world, or even yourself if that is needed for your healing. Spend time each day in the practice of generating loving, compassionate feelings in your heart. Bit by bit they will grow more powerful until they become a tangible force you can create at will for the benefit of others and to direct toward any situation on the planet.

Feelings amplify the power of thought. If the results you are seeking seem to elude you, then amplify your feelings.

Believing

Christ said, "Whatsoever you pray for, believing you have already received, will be granted to you," regardless of whether it's a spiritual or material goal.

There we have the key—believing we already have it. But how do we believe something when our eyes are telling us otherwise? We believe we have already received it by feeling it. Feel with all five senses, whether it's a tangible object like a car or an intangible one like good health. If we're repeating mantras with a feeling of "not yet manifest," we will be creating a lot more that is not yet manifest! The result remains perpetually in the future, just beyond our grasp.

When I'm working on manifesting a car, for example, I *see* it in my driveway, I *feel* myself driving it, I *sense* myself vacuuming the upholstery, sudsing the hubcaps, wiping the windows, playing with the keys. I *hear* the sounds, *smell* the smells and get all my senses involved.

I never merely picture my desired car parked by the curb because the universe then may simply produce someone with that vehicle parked there! It's crucial to add detailed feelings of personal ownership. It's also important to ask for our prayers and desires to manifest only in accordance with the will of God and divine selection. The Divine may even send something better or more suitable for our needs.

Feelings Are Magnets

Feelings are magnets that attract similar feelings to us. If we are depressed because of debt, a leaky roof, car repairs and so on, we attract more problems because, as Gregg Braden explained in *The God Code*, the universe doesn't understand the word "don't." Our feelings are direct commands to the universe, so never, ever spend time revolving thoughts and feelings about what you don't want—the word "don't" will be deleted!

In *The I Am Discourses, Vol. 3*, Saint Germain says we can precipitate anything whatsoever on which we hold our creative thought and feeling while steadfastly ignoring all outer appearances to the contrary. Put a big mental X over those unwanted outer conditions and then refuse to give them any attention, because what you focus your attention on expands in your life. Keep your attention on what you want. (The average attention span of seven seconds is too short to sustain the vision of what we desire to manifest.)

Jump-start positive feelings with positive body language. The famous success coach Tony Robbins teaches that we can quickly change how we feel by changing our physiology, so smile and hold your head high. Assume the body language of happiness and your feelings will follow. In my DVD workshop, "Acting Skills for Singers," I teach that feelings and body language are much bigger factors in singing success than voice. The same is true for other performing arts and in your visualizations.

Feelings can turn our words from rote repetition to powerful commands to the universe. Their frequencies also vibrate in the non-local quantum level where everything is connected. As author Lynn Grabhorn put it, "No feel, no get!"

I have recently discovered that it's much easier to switch to positive feelings by using positive questions rather than positive statements. The cynical part of the conscious mind, the left brain, can refute statements, but when they're put in a question format, both the conscious and subconscious get busy to produce the answer. Here are some examples:

Why is it so easy for me to:

- feel happy all day?

- feel prosperous and abundant?

- make good food choices?

- spend my income so wisely?

- increase my income each month?

- be so loving and kind?

- remain healthy and slender?

- use my time so efficiently?

Revolving these kind of questions in my mind, instead of statements or negative thought loops, has been very successful for me. Formulate questions to suit your particular needs and goals. Don't think about the answers—that's the job for your subconscious.

The goal here is to generate positive feelings and to see our intentions as already existing. As our powers of manifestation are accelerating at this time, it's doubly important to control our thoughts and feelings. We become what we focus our attention upon, "What the eye beholds, the soul unfolds."

A large percentage of people are unable to recreate some of the positive feelings necessary for manifestation because they have never experienced them. In *ThetaHealing*, Vianna Stibal says that when you enter the slow theta brainwaves, you can ask the Creator to download the desired feelings into your cells, whether joy, self-confidence, self-esteem or whatever. Her techniques can be applied to other goals like healing or eliminating negative beliefs.

When Our Desires Are Not Fulfilled

Sometimes we get what we want and sometimes we don't. Yet we always get what is needed for our inner growth, woven in with what others need for their growth. Our higher self has an agenda for our evolution that supersedes our human desires. Our environment is a reflection of our vibration and level of consciousness, so the faster we learn and grow, the more opportunities appear and the more old paradigms fall away. When our goals are aligned with our spiritual curriculum, everything we need shows up on schedule. Mark Prophet said that all experiences are for the education of the soul, to teach it the meaning of love.

If we insist on getting what we want, we also get everything that goes with it. Whenever I have doggedly persisted in forcing something into my life in spite of hints from the universe, I always ended up regretting it later when all the attendant problems showed up with it.

Our karma can also stand in the way of achieving some of our goals. For example, if we burned a village in a past embodiment, destroying other people's homes, we may have endless trouble acquiring or keeping a home in this life if that karma has not been transmuted and is now coming due. All the more reason to cancel these energy records with the frequencies of Kuan Yin mantras. The mantras from the Summit Lighthouse at the end of Chapter 22 are also excellent for this.

Another cause for non-manifestation of our desires is if we are motivated by fear or desperation. This underlying energy can short-circuit all our efforts and we attract more fear and desperation in our circumstances. What we resist persists. It's better to simply remove our attention from what we don't want and it will eventually fade out of our lives.

CHAPTER 12 ~ **Entities & Non-Physical Beings**

When we study the ancient texts of Avalokitesvara (Kuan Yin), we occasionally find mention of demons, ghosts and hellish realms, along with the recommended reciting of the mantras and sutras for protection from these dark forces. As we saw in Chapter 4, the Lotus Sutra says that tormenting spirits and demons are unable to harm anyone who they hear sincerely calling upon the name of Kuan Yin.

Are these denizens of the underworld real? Some people think they are projections from the unconscious; others think they are archetypes or symbols. According to most spiritual traditions, they are indeed real and the war between the legions of Light and the hordes of darkness is not just a metaphor—at least not in this dimensional octave that we inhabit. Baudelaire once said that "the greatest trick of the devil was convincing the world that he doesn't exist."

According to the *Karandavyuha Sutra*, Kuan Yin's infinite compassion extends to the dark realms, too, for the freeing of those inhabitants who are ready to turn and serve the Light. The time has arrived for knowledge of this area to become mainstream once again, just as angels have, and tools will be given in this chapter for dealing with these situations. If it makes you uncomfortable, then you can skip this section and move on to Chapter 13.

The American Psychiatric Association recognizes a condition known as Dissociative Trance Disorder, which includes Possessive Trance. This is characterized by the appearance of alternate identities of possessing agents like entities, spirits or demons. Some of the symptoms of pathological possession may include bizarre, cruel, self-destructive, dangerous, extreme or criminal behavior, enormous strength, eating materials like metal, frequent foul language, multiple personalities, uncontrollable urges, anger, addictions and trashing one's environment. The list of addictions and behaviors caused or incited by entities or demons would cover several pages. Any obsessive or fanatical behavior could be an indication of other non-physical beings in the body. Innocuous behaviors and habits that are not part of the host's usual identity can be another sign. This could be a desire for certain foods, clothing or different sexual activity. Many of these entities are described in *The Path To Immortality* by Mark L. Prophet

Some psychiatrists, therapists and hypnotherapists have practices that include the removal of entities from their clients. The attached spirit sometimes first reveals itself during an appointment and its removal invariably ends the physical, mental or emotional problem for which the client was seeking treatment, including long-standing physical diseases. Dr. William J. Baldwin's *Healing Lost Souls* and Dr. Shakuntala Modi's *Remarkable Healings* are both excellent books on this subject if you wish to delve into it in greater depth.

It is interesting to note that in the past, when it was culturally understood that some diseases were caused by an invading spirit, the host was frequently healed when a shaman or other healer released the spirit. In the New Testament, Christ cast out devils and unclean spirits. He asked the demon in a possessed man, "What is your name?" and the response was, "My name is Legion, for we are many" [Luke 8:30; Mark 5:9]. Today, psychiatrists also ask the attached spirit to identify itself and often find there are several. Deliverance Ministries and other pentecostal or charismatic movements have been a resurging phenomenon for decades.

When I was about twenty-two years old and living in Los Angeles, I had a second job doing childcare for a man who worked at night. I remember one evening he had a few beers and started acting abnormally. Soon he began growling and making strange guttural sounds. Then he started prowling and throwing things. Instinctively I called his mother who lived nearby. When I approached the exit door, I turned my head just in time to avoid the heavy mug that smashed against the door. As I was leaving, his mother arrived with two men carrying bibles and they immediately began an exorcism. Apparently, this had happened before. Unfortunately, at that time I did not know about calling to Archangel Michael or Kuan Yin for protection.

Different Types of Spirits

"Spirit attachment" is a blanket term that can refer to a number of different types of nonphysical beings. Some healers and therapists, including William J. Baldwin, Ph.D., have categorized them roughly as follows:

- **Discarnate or Earthbound Soul**: a human spirit that has lost its body in death and not moved on into the Light.

- **Devil or Demon**: a dark-force being, allied with the forces opposed to Light and Love.

- **Entity**: a being formed from addictive energies that become a separate type of life-form that then perpetuates the craving or behavior. (An entity can also be a life form from another dimension that got trapped here accidentally.)

- **Soul Parts of Others**.

Discarnates can enter accidentally or intentionally. A person whose physical body has died is intended to go to the Light, but a few people become confused and enter someone else instead, often the nearest person. This can happen anywhere but is especially common in hospitals, battlefields, disaster areas, accident sites, cemeteries, bars and casinos.

Some people go to the lower astral or dark realms instead of the Light. One of my friends told me about her criminal brother-in-law who was clinically dead for some time before being resuscitated. He clearly remembered being taken to horror chambers of classical hellish descriptions and being subjected to excruciating torture. After coming back to his body, he vowed to give up his life of crime and drug pushing. Unfortunately, he didn't keep his vow.

My grandmother remembers watching a cruel woman on her deathbed in Yugoslavia screaming that devils were taking her to the darkness.

Meeting a Devil

My first conscious experience with a dark being occurred at the age of sixteen. In the predawn twilight I suddenly became aware of something looking through the window over my bed. I saw a stereotypical black devil and felt a palpable evil presence that filled me with the utmost horror. I was soaked in cold sweat when it left. Believe me, it was not a metaphor.

Others have told me of similar experiences. An actor in Sydney, Australia, said the devil he saw was red, and the awareness of being in a truly evil presence was terrifying beyond all description.

You can train yourself to call to Archangel Michael whenever you find yourself in a dangerous or evil situation, even during your sleep. When I'm asleep, I wake up back in my body as soon as I call his name.

Many saints, like Padre Pio and the *Curé d'Ars* (Saint John Vianney), have in their biographies stories of being tormented and physically attacked by devils. These dark-force beings have numerous ways of either entering or latching onto people. They look for any breaks or weaknesses in a person's aura or electromagnetic field and slide in. These rents can be caused by extreme stress or trauma, anesthetics, jagged rhythms of sound or music, profanity, sexual abuse or promiscuity, drugs, alcohol, intense negative emotions, especially fear or anger, and numerous other ways including dabbling in the occult. Once entered, the demon remains a well-concealed cause of violence, verbal abuse, accidents, crime, self-destructive behavior, and turning away from one's mission or path in life.

A former co-worker, Michaela, once had several people at her home as dinner guests. During the course of the meal she looked up at the man across the table and saw a devil appearing in him, red eyes and all. As she stared dumbfounded, she realized by his return gaze that he knew he was being discovered. She was later able to warn his partner to cancel all business dealings with him.

Addiction entities can cause us endless trouble with smoking, alcohol, drugs, sex, anger, sugar cravings, uncontrollable desires and dozens of other

86

problems. Clairvoyants sometimes see these creatures siphoning off the light and energy of the host and causing further unwanted cravings. The entity causing nicotine addiction has been seen as resembling a huge six-foot tobacco worm. Others may look like insects, but they can be any form or even formless. This is one reason why it's so difficult to break addictive cravings.

Unless we work diligently to daily be filled with spiritual light, most of us will have some attached spirits or entities of one kind or another. It seems to be a part of the human condition. Freeing them and ourselves usually involves angelic or divine intervention. Many enlightened psychiatrists and other therapists who work in this area will ask for the assistance of protecting angels, clean-up angels and Archangel Michael. They request permission to proceed from the person's higher self and work with the attached spirits one at a time, convincing them to leave voluntarily and be escorted by angels to their right place in the Light. (This system works just as well for those who feel they are working with archetypes or subconscious symbols.) They should never be just ruthlessly cast out or they will either return or enter another. These beings need loving assistance just like other forms of life.

When the host person is cleared, both the therapist and client should do the prayer work to invoke divine light to fill all spaces within and around themselves and seal their auric field with a shield of light. It is good daily practice to invoke the light's cleansing and protective powers. This can be done quickly and easily with intention, visualization and verbal command.

My Haunted House

When I bought a house in 1995, I went there at nights to clean and paint before moving in. Every night I heard footsteps coming down from the attic, someone seemed to be following me and trying to push me off my painting chair. I kept all the lights on and never turned my back to the doorway even when washing brushes in the bathtub. Each night I fled as fast as I could when my work was done. Then I hired a painter to do the attic rooms, and after a few days he nervously said, "There's a ghost or something in that house, that follows me. I hear footsteps coming downstairs. It seems to want to push me and make me fall while I'm working. I don't dare turn my back to the doorway, even when I'm washing paintbrushes in the bathtub!"

Then I knew it wasn't my imagination, as he had the identical experiences. When I told an acquaintance I had bought the green house by the railroad tracks she said, "Oh, I looked through that house when it was for sale. I got the feeling it was haunted by someone in the attic. Have you told him to go to the Light and asked for Archangel Michael's help?"

Yes, indeed I had. Whenever I worked in the attic rooms I told whoever it was that he needed to go with the angels and that I was the new owner and would take good care of this house. I also did a series of prayers to Archangel Michael, mantras to Kuan Yin, and went through each room and the spooky basement twirling my stainless-steel sword in every direction and into every nook and cranny. Shortly after I moved in, the house felt clear and I never again heard footsteps coming down the stairs at night.

A stainless-steel knife or sword can cut through the lower-dimensional astral plane and its denizens. They will flee whenever you use one with this intent. Many people I know keep a small steak knife just for this purpose. They use it to cut around themselves, family members (with permission and carefully), pets, vehicles, all through their homes, and even in hospital and motel rooms (when no one is looking). We can also use it to cut around photos of loved ones. Ask Archangel Michael to place his blue-flame sword over your knife and to do the work with you. Be very careful—my sword once flew out of my hand and just missed my dog. Another time, my knife hit my ankle as I was cutting around myself. There's no need to make contact—a few inches or more away is fine. (Note that for the user's protection the sword or knife does not have to be sharpened. It is the nature of the steel itself that repels the entities.) You can also wield a sword for long distance work, visualizing as you work while reciting prayers or mantras for protection.

Constantly call to Archangel Michael, Legions of Light and Kuan Yin when doing knife work, and request that entities and beings who are removed be escorted to higher dimensional octaves for healing, or to whatever is the right place for them at this time. When you're done, ask angels to fill with light all gaps and spaces in yourself, in others and in every place you have cleared. This is to prevent new dark energies from moving in.

Now you know why Avalokitesvara sometimes spoke of this subject. It affects all of us whether we are aware of it or not. The entities and demons of the unseen astral plane need "food" to survive as well. Having no direct access to divine light as we do, they must feed on the misqualified light that we produce through our negative thoughts, feelings, habits and deeds. The more of this substance we produce in our daily lives, the more these entities will be drawn to us like moths to a flame. That's why we all need to purify our auras with the protective power of daily prayer, meditation and mantra.

CHAPTER 13 ~ **Miracles, Miracles, Miracles!**

There are countless testimonials that testify to Kuan Yin's merciful intercession. In Taiwan and China, temples distribute books of miracle stories written by Chinese compilers. The locals have them memorized through oral tradition. Some of these records are seventeen centuries old, while other events have occurred in modern times. Most of the recipients of divine intervention had chanted devotions to either the masculine embodiment of divine compassion, Avalokitesvara, or to the feminine emanations, Kuan Yin or Tara.

One of the oldest stories tells about Chang. His neighbor's house had caught on fire and the wind was blowing toward Chang's home. Instead of gathering up belongings and fleeing, he and his family chanted the Kuan Yin sutra. Just as the fire reached his fence, the wind reversed direction and the fire died. Some local neighbors mocked the miracle, saying it was pure luck. So on another hot, windy day, they tossed firebrands on Chang's roof and each one harmlessly died out. Then they finally believed.

Another devotee always wore a tiny Kuan Yin statue in his hair behind his neck. (This was a common practice in earlier times.) When he was to be beheaded, the executioner's blade broke on his neck three times. His life was then spared. Later he noticed three cuts on the neck of his tiny statue where the Bodhisattva had taken the blows for him.

In the thirteenth century, Grand Marshall Fan, who had diseased eyes, sent his son to P'u-T'o Shan. His son prayed at the Cave of Tidal Sounds and brought home some of the water. Fan's eyes were cured when he washed them in the water. He sent his son back to the cave to give gratitude, whereupon Kuan Yin appeared to him wearing a cape of light. He saw her again at Sudana's Rock wearing a white robe.

In another story, a merchant was on his way to make a pilgrimage to Kuan Yin's island. As he was about to embark on his ship, a messenger ran up and told him a fire was burning next to his store. The merchant refused to turn back, determined to finish his journey. When he returned from P'u-T'o, he found his building had been saved while all those around it had been totally destroyed by the fire.

One of the most famous Kuan Yin legends is about an emperor who loved to eat clams. One day his chef could not open a particularly large one. When the emperor heard of this, he went and prayed to this unusual clam. It opened by itself and inside was an image of Kuan Yin. He then vowed mercy to all living creatures and never ate clams again.

Another old story tells of a man whose feet became paralyzed, so he started chanting Kuan Yin's sutra daily. After three years, a monk appeared to him while he was chanting. When the man asked for the reason behind his paralysis, the monk replied that it was karma for capturing and binding living beings in a previous life. The monk told him to close his eyes. He did so and felt a six-inch nail being pulled out of each knee. He was then healed and recognized the monk as Kuan Yin. Because of his devotions, decades of karma had been reduced to three years.

Miraculous Kuan Yin. The story goes that a traveler was taking a picture of clouds and this beautiful image appeared as the film was being developed

In more recent times, a woman devotee was waiting for a ferry in order to cross a wide river. As she was about to embark, Kuan Yin appeared and warned her with a hand signal not to board the craft. The woman decided to wait, and later the ferry sank as it was crossing the river.

Many sailors have reported seeing Kuan Yin's image during bad storms. In each case they followed her to safety through treacherous waters.

In *Bodhisattva of Compassion*, John Blofeld recounts the story of a terminally ill young Chinese man who was lying in a coma. His relatives all gathered to recite the Dharani Sutra. Near midnight, he suddenly awoke and exclaimed, "Look at that girl!" A few people saw a young woman in flowing robes sitting on the high rafters. She held a vase with liquid light, Kuan Yin's nectar of compassion, which she sprinkled down onto the young man. She then miraculously vanished and he was completely recovered within 48 hours.

One group of devotees traveled across territory occupied by marauding outlaws, but were not attacked. Later when the bandits' leader was asked why they had not attacked the group, he replied, "We only saw a herd of deer pass by on the road."

During World War II, when Taiwan was bombed, many people saw Kuan Yin appear in the sky as a young woman catching bombs in her robes so they would not explode. I recently met Master Lu, a monk from Taiwan, who was born next door to a Kuan Yin temple where she was seen catching a bomb. Especially during times of national danger, it is recommended to daily use the mantra: *I take refuge in Kuan Yin of the vajra pestle hand*, for the protection against enemies. The Chinese pronunciation is: *Nahmo jing gahg chew show Gwun Yin*. You just may save your country. (The other versions of these mantras are included in Chapter 22.)

In 1922, a massive earthquake in Asakusa, Tokyo, caused a great firestorm when buildings collapsed and cook stoves overturned. People fled to ponds in the parks but still succumbed to the wind-driven flames. Thousands crowded into a Kannon (Kuan Yin) Temple built in the 7th century by fishermen who found her statue in their nets. The people chanted her mantras continuously and every time the flames gusted toward the wooden temple, an opposing gust would reverse the fire's direction back onto itself. All those in the building were saved and many saw Kannon riding on a dragon's head. This temple is still standing today.

One couple in Montana went to spend a three-day weekend at a camp near Phillipsburg to look for gemstones. They used the mantra for finding treasures in the earth. Their other camp mates found some small gems, but this couple found a lot more, including a large, rare, pink sapphire. The mantra is: "I take refuge in Kuan Yin of the jeweled-chest hand," pronounced: *Nahmo you-eh foo show Gwun Yin*.

Years ago, one of my friends was unjustly fired from her job. When her employer, also a Kuan Yin devotee, was about to go on stage to deliver a lecture, Kuan Yin appeared there and barred the entrance until my friend was rehired.

A friend from Sweden wanted to immigrate to the United States. The quota at that time had already been filled, but she had faith in Kuan Yin's power. She did mantra #27 from the Thirty-Three Manifestations 144,000 times in one week. Then she did the entire *Kuan Yin's Crystal Rosary* (a very long one from The Summit Lighthouse, see Internet Resources in the back) as a novena for forty-three days. On the thirty-third day, Kuan Yin appeared to her and told her she would get her wish if she did not doubt the appearance. On the forty-third day, she received her miracle in the form of a letter from immigration officials. It was dated the thirty-third day of her rosary vigil.

A couple of years ago, I spent an entire day chanting several of the 33 mantras while hiking in the woods with my dog, Nike. When I was descending the mountain at the day's end, I noticed my body and clothing had been transformed into the likeness of the antique wooden Kuan Yin in my home, even to the tiny details of peeling gold paint on her arms and robes. The Bodhisattva's presence visibly overshadowed me until the end of the trail. I was also freed from an addiction after doing The Great Compassion Mantra five times a day for about one year. (For some people it takes less time, for others it takes longer.) Kuan Yin has also helped me with the buying and selling of property.

David Milak, owner of the Sacred Mysteries Bookstore in Livingston, Montana, had a booth at a local fair. He had some large antique Kuan Yin and Tara statues on display throughout the event. On the last day of the fair, a mother and her child visited the booth, admiring an ivory Kuan Yin. After they left, the clairvoyant in the next booth excitedly exclaimed to him, "Did you SEE that?"

"See what?" he asked.

"Rainbow-colored light came pouring out from that statue, enveloping that woman, her child and you!"

Another friend of mine wrote a letter to the Karmic Board (earth's spiritual overseers) and burned the letter in front of the Kuan Yin statue in her yard. In the letter she was requesting much needed help with her move to another house. She got a phone call the very next morning from an out-of-state friend who said, "Kuan Yin just told me that I should come down and help you." (Burning a letter written to a spiritual being is one way of communicating with spirit. I burn mine in the wood stove or the kitchen sink.)

Another miracle recently occurred when a woman who is a long-time devotee erected a large statue of Kuan Yin among the tall junipers on a hill in a pasture. Shortly after the statue was set in place, the woman was walking back to her car when she had a sudden irresistible urge to return to the statue. As she approached it, there was an overwhelming sense of a tangible presence. She knelt down, reached out to touch the arm and was startled to feel soft, warm flesh. Even though the statue was cast in cement, it felt like an actual person standing there. She realized that Kuan Yin had overshadowed the statue to radiate energies to the world and to those who would approach this image and touch it, even if they only felt the cement.

Kuan Yin has cured many illnesses, prevented car accidents, averted financial crises, repaired reputations, protected homes and jobs, and helped with legal problems. I had just about finished the manuscript for this book when I met 28-year-old Miles from Livingston and heard his amazing story:

Miles had been on heavy opiates for pain after a car crash. A drug counselor had him on benzodiazepine (a Valium-type antidepressant), but Miles found this to be even worse. He happened upon the Sacred Mysteries Bookstore where he discovered the Kuan Yin and Tara Mantras. He decided on a natural detoxification program including intense meditation, yoga, deep breathing, a vegan diet, Ayurvedics, reciting mantras and spiritual study. He particularly focused on the mantras given in Chapter 1, and begged and implored Tara and Kuan Yin to release him from his suffering and cravings.

One day, a few weeks before I met him, he had an intense desire for benzodiazepine, but he took a stand and refused to give in. The moment he made this decision, there was a great burst of light above him and Kuan Yin appeared seated on her lotus throne. She was about eight feet tall and dressed in blues and violets. She descended in a blaze of light, surrounded by the swirling elements of fire, air, water, earth and ether, which were curling and cascading all around her.

He was sitting in a chair at the time and she descended into him in the lotus posture, infusing and surrounding his being. He was filled with ecstasy and infinite love beyond all comprehension. In full, lucid awareness, he was shown the entire universe with all its dimensions. He was shown that the earth dimension is a place to learn and that it is holographic in nature. He was shown celestial beings, spirits, the nature of stars, and he understood it all for a short while.

When he began returning to body consciousness, he realized he had stopped breathing. "Breathe, my son," said her voice from within. He felt so loved, he began repeating, "I love you, I love you." Then his hand floated up as though guided by an inner arm, and touched the side of his nose that had a double piercing. Because it had been the gift of a recently deceased friend, he was quite attached to it. Yet he sensed that the message of the touch was, "Take that out for now, you don't need it, have non-attachment."

His head had fallen back in ecstasy, and now normalized its position. He saw a ball of fiery *chi* force, and Kuan Yin moved his hands to hold it, making flowing *Tai Chi* movements. Then his girlfriend entered the room and the voice said, "You have to go back now. Rest, my son." The experience ended. He went to his altar and bowed down repeating, "Thank you, thank you."

Miles feels that this divine visitation was bestowed upon him as a reinforcement and confirmation of his decision not to take the drug, and to fight his battle from a spiritual level—and, no doubt, as a reward for his intense devotion and mantras to Kuan Yin.

~ PART III ~
Miracle Mantras & Powerful Meditations

Kuan Yin
Who Holds the Sutras

CHAPTER 14 ~ **The Great Compassion Dharani Sutra**
(Da Bei Zhou/Karuna Dharani)

What is a Dharani Sutra? A sutra is a spiritual discourse spoken by a Buddha. Dharani is a Sanskrit word meaning to unify, maintain or hold, and refers to a long series of powerful syllables used as mantras. It is a tool or receptacle for retaining concepts or experience. A dharani is longer than a normal mantra. Many of its syllables have no meaning as word or symbol, but instead, the sounds encode an energy essence that release specific physical and spiritual frequencies. This is in agreement with the quantum theory that everything is a wave frequency that can be affected by other frequencies, including sound.

In this chapter the terms dharani and mantra are used interchangeably and refer to the 84- line Great Compassion Dharani Mantra revealed in this sutra. (It is sometimes written in a 42-line format.) In Chinese it is known as the *Da Bei Zhou* or the *Ta Pei Chou* (*Ta Pei* means greatly pitying). In India, it is called the *Maha Karuna* (Great Compassion) Dharani. It is said to be one of the most powerful ways of invoking Kuan Yin, and for one's consciousness to soar to realms of light. Like other sacred texts, there are many levels of interpretation.

The Great Compassion Dharani Sutra was given by Kuan Yin (as Avolokitesvara) to the world in order that "living beings may obtain peace and joy, be healed of illness, have long life, enjoy prosperity, erase the evil karma of sin and offenses, remove hardship and suffering, and especially to increase spiritual attainment and virtue."

The ancient teaching is that receiving the gift of The Great Compassion Mantra given in this sutra is an exceedingly rare opportunity extended only to those who have earned it in the past. Finding it has been compared to finding the rarest and most valuable of jewels.

The Repentance Ritual

During the Tang dynasty (AD 618–907) there were several Chinese translations of the Dharani made from the Indian Sanskrit version, most notably by Shramana Bhagavadharma and Amoghavajra. Currently, there are several versions available in Sanskrit and Chinese on the Internet, as well as some English translations.

Parts of this sutra are incorporated in the text of The Ritual of Great Compassion Repentance, which is popular in temples in Taiwan, China and some Asian communities in America. Late in the tenth century, when the original manual for this repentance ritual, which lasts two-to-three hours, was created by the patriarch Chih-li, the sutra had already been popular for a long time and was chanted for many different purposes. The current repentance manual based on Chih-li's version is probably several hundred years old.

It begins with invocations to Kuan Yin, many Buddhas, Maitreya, Manjushri, and other celestial beings. There are offerings of incense and flowers, recitations of the Dharani, the Ten Vows, chanting the Kuan Yin mantra, making confession and singing. In part of the Repentance Ritual, which is always led by a "master of repentance," the congregation moves around the room in a choreographed, serpentine pattern while chanting *"Kuan Yin Pu'sa"* (Kuan Yin Bodhisattva).

Many people bring water bottles so they can bring home "mantra water" afterwards for healing purposes. Skeptical smirks are decreasing now that Japanese researcher Masaru Emoto has photographed and documented the effects of positive words, prayers, sounds and images on water crystals, changing them into patterns of great beauty. You can make your own mantra water by repeating the Dharani (given in the next chapter) five times over clean water.

The Sutra & Its Promises

The following is a condensed recapitulation of The Great Compassion Dharani Sutra:

Thus I have heard, at one time the Sakyamuni Buddha lived at the palace of the One Who Regards the Sounds of the World on Potala Mountain. A great assembly of Buddhas, Bodhisattvas, Mahasattvas, celestial beings, gods and goddesses, elemental kings, nature spirits and so forth were gathered there.

The Avalokitesvara (Kuan Yin) who was among them, secretly emitted great spiritual light, and instantly illuminated all ten directions and the entire 3,000 world system. The Dharani King Bodhisattva asked the Buddha to reveal who had performed this enormous feat.

The Buddha responded that the Bodhisattva-Mahasattva Who Regards the Worlds Sounds had done this to comfort all living beings.

Then Avalokitesvara spoke, saying,

"I have a Great Compassion Heart Dharani Mantra, which I wish to put forth for the happiness of all living beings, so they may have long lives of health, prosperity and virtue, protection from all forms of disasters, and eradication of all evil karma and sins.

Many eons ago I was given this Dharani Mantra by a Buddha named Thousand Ray King in Stillness. It was to be used for the benefit of all especially during the evil times of the future [our modern era]. I then vowed to benefit all living beings and received 1,000 hands and 1,000 eyes to assist my work. All the innumerable Buddhas heard, accepted and maintained this Dharani Mantra since that time, and I have always recited it. One who holds this mantra by regular recitation and by keeping the Code of Conduct is reborn in the higher worlds.

The Ten Vows

Those who wish to recite it should first evoke in their hearts compassion for all creatures and recite these Ten Vows. [You may substitute "Hail" for Namo, and Kuan Yin for Avalokitesvara. A more extended variation of Kuan Yin's Ten Vows is included as Part I of the Thirty-Three Miracle Mantras Ritual in Chapter 21.]

1) Namo compassionate Avalokitesvara,
   May I swiftly know all Dharmas!

2) Namo compassionate Avalokitesvara,
   May I rapidly attain the Wisdom Eye!

3) Namo compassionate Avalokitesvara,
   May I swiftly liberate all beings!

4) Namo compassionate Avalokitesvara,
   May I rapidly attain skillful methods to teach and enlighten!

5) Namo compassionate Avalokitesvara,
   May I swiftly embark the Prajna Wisdom boat!

6) Namo compassionate Avalokitesvara,
   May I rapidly rise out of the ocean of suffering!

7) Namo compassionate Avalokitesvara,
   May I swiftly achieve good morals, samadhi and the Way!

8) Namo compassionate Avalokitesvara,
   May I rapidly climb Nirvana Mountain!

9) Namo compassionate Avalokitesvara,
   May I swiftly be in the unconditioned existence!

10) Namo compassionate Avalokitesvara,
    May I rapidly be united with the Dharma-Nature Body!

While reciting this Dharani:

If I face the mountain of knives, may it shatter itself.

If I face boiling oil, may it dry up.

If I face hells, may they vanish.

If I face the Hungry Ghosts, may they be satiated.

If I face the Asura demons, may their evilness be tamed.

If I face animals, may they become wise.

After making the vows, sincerely recite my name and that of my teacher Amitabha. Then recite this Dharani five times per evening to erase millions of eons of negative karma.

The Promises

All who recite and hold this mantra are protected from knives, boiling oil, hell, ghosts and demons. They will give wisdom even to animals, take rebirth in whatever Buddha land [spiritual plane] they desire, and obtain the fruits of what they seek in this life.

Cast out all that is unwholesome and impure. And remember, *the promised results will not occur if there lingers any doubt.*

All offenses will be erased when one sincerely recites The Great Compassion Dharani with faith, even the ten evils (killing, stealing, sexual misconduct, greed, hate, stupidity, irresponsible speech, including condemnation, swearing and gossip, lies, verbal abuse, deceitful speech); and the five rebellious acts (murdering father, murdering mother, murdering an arhat, shedding a Buddha's blood, and causing disharmony in the spiritual community). Also wiped away are the offenses of slandering people and spiritual teachings, breaking rules of pure eating (only vegetarian food with no alliums: onions, garlic, chives, shallots, leeks); and breaking the five basic precepts: no killing, no stealing, no lying, criticism or harsh speech, no misuse of sexual energy, and no alcohol, drugs or nicotine). The only exception is doubt. If one doubts the mantra, not even slight offenses will be eradicated.

Those who recite The Great Compassion Mantra with belief and sincerity will not suffer any of the 15 kinds of bad death, even if one is a soldier. They will also obtain the 15 kinds of good birth. They will have abundance, protection and awaken to the profound meaning of the Dharma [Spiritual Teaching]. Constantly recite and hold this Dharani Mantra."

The Bodhisattva Who Regards The Worlds Sounds (Kuan Yin) then recited the 84 sentences of the mantra. [These are included in Chapter 15.] When it was finished, the earth shook and jeweled flowers rained down from the sky. All the Buddhas of the ten directions were delighted, but the demons, evil spirits and evil practitioners became extremely fearful. Everyone in the congregation attained a higher spiritual level.

Then the Brahma King rose and said to Avalokitesvara, "I have attended countless Buddha assemblies and heard innumerable Dharmas and Dharanis, but never have I heard anything like this. Please explain the character of this Dharani."

Avalokitesvara replied:

"It is the Ten Hearts:

1) The merciful and compassionate heart

2) The impartial heart

3) The unconditioned and still heart

4) The pure and unattached heart

5) The emptiness-contemplation heart

6) The respectful heart

102

7) The humble heart

8) The simple unconfused heart

9) The no-view and non-grasping heart

10) The highest enlightened Bodhi heart

"Those who recite and hold this holy Dharani should keep the five precepts of good conduct and the rules of pure eating. They should have an impartial, merciful heart to all living beings and always recite the Dharani. They should bathe, retire to a clean room, wear clean clothing and adorn their prayer altars. They should light candles and offer incense, flowers, fruits and vegetables. Then keeping the mind still and one-pointed, recite this mantra.

"I will illumine and protect these devotees, and they will be cured of illness. If they develop a compassionate heart to all living creatures, I will command the various celestial beings and elemental spirits of nature to protect them. Recite this mantra if you are lost in the mountains, or encounter dangerous beasts or snakes. Recite it when besieged by soldiers, robbers or criminals. Use it when arrested or imprisoned, and for protection against black magic or hexes. Say the mantra in childbirth and during epidemics.

"Recite the mantra to cleanse yourself of untoward sexual desire, sexual addictions and the karma of misuse of sexual energies. [These include oral and unmarried sex, adultery, masturbation, etc. See the note at the end of this chapter on how energy records can be cleared and erased, especially with the violet light and the use of these mantras.]

"Recite the mantra five times while making five colored threads (blue, red, white, black and yellow) into a lasso. Recite the mantra 21 times while tying 21 knots in it. Wear it around your neck. Cultivate the six perfections of morality, generosity, patience, vigor, meditation and wisdom.

"This mantra has been recited in the past by millions of Buddhas for the progress and advancement of living beings on their spiritual path. Those on the three evil paths who reside in the dark regions can be released from suffering after hearing this mantra.

"If anyone seeks to attain his wishes, he should keep the precepts and the code of conduct, including those of pure eating, and recite the Dharani for 21 days. Then he can obtain his desire [when the timing is right] and erase negative karma. If a devotee who recites and holds the mantra walks in the wind, then persons downwind have karma erased if they are touched by the same wind that touched the devotee.

"The blessings, virtues and karmic repayments accruing to those who regularly recite and hold the mantra are inconceivable. Their words are respected and they are loved by the countless enlightened ones. They are beacons of light to the world and they constantly use this Dharani to rescue living beings and to heal diseases.

"To secure the boundary of your property, recite the Dharani 21 times over a knife, then mark the ground with it, or recite the Dharani 21 times over clean water and sprinkle it on the the four directions of your boundary.

"If anyone even just hears the full name of this Dharani: *The Sutra of the Vast, Great, Perfect, Full, Unimpeded Great Compassion Heart Dharani of the Thousand-Handed, Thousand-Eyed Bodhisattva Who Regards the World's Sounds*, his heavy karma of eons will be eradicated, so how much more for those who recite and hold it! Those who find and hold this Dharani have already made offerings, penances and planted virtuous roots in their past lives. Those who for the purpose of saving living beings from suffering, recite and hold the mantra according to the teachings, have achieved The Great Compassion and will soon be a buddha, a fully enlightened being.

"He who recites the mantra for all living creatures he sees, so that it is heard by them and causes their enlightenment, his merit and virtue are immeasurable.

"If you apply yourself, remain vegetarian, keep all the codes of conduct, refrain from drugs and alcohol, forsake and repent of all prior sins on behalf of all living beings, not just for self interest, if you confess your bad deeds of all past ages and sincerely recite the Dharani steadily and flowingly without interruption, you will achieve the four fruits of Shramana (*arhatship*), attain wisdom and the ten levels of Bodhisattvahood. You will receive all you seek."

At this point in the Sutra, Sakyamuni Buddha says to Ananda,

"In times of national disaster or difficulty, if the nation's king is kind and compassionate to people and animals, governs justly, and for seven days and nights recites and holds this Great Compassion Heart Dharani Mantra with physical and mental diligence, all his nation's disasters will be erased. It will be a prosperous and peaceful country.

"If any catastrophes, invasions, epidemics, drought, floods, treasons or other problems beset your country, make an image [traditionally painted on white wool or cotton] of the Thousand-Eyed Bodhisattva Kuan Yin and set it facing west. Make offerings before it of various types of flowers, fragrances, incense, banners, precious canopies, vegetables, fruits and drinks. If the king recites and holds the sacred phrases of this Dharani with sincerity and diligence, these problems will disappear, crops will be plentiful and the citizens happy."

Ananda asked, "What is the name of this mantra? How should we accept and hold it?"

The Buddha replied, "This Holy Mantra has many names. One is Vast, Great, Perfect, Full. It is also called the Dharani of Relieving Suffering, The Dharani of Lengthening Life, The Dharani of Destroying Evil Karmic Obstacles, The Dharani of Quickly Attaining a Higher Level. This is how you should accept and hold it."

Ananda then asked, "What is the name of the Bodhisattva-Mahasattva who gave this Dharani?"

The Buddha said, "This Bodhisattva is called Avalokitesvara, also named Twirling a Lasso, also A Thousand Luminous Eyes. Eons ago, this one became a Buddha named True Dharma Brightness Tathagata. All celestial beings and all mankind should always make offerings to this one and recite his name devotedly, thereby receiving countless blessings, wiping out countless sins and achieving rebirth in the paradise of the Pure Land of Amitabha... If you wish to invite this Bodhisattva to visit, recite the mantra 21 times over Guggula [Parthian] incense and burn it."

[Next in the Sutra are a number of remedies with unusual ingredients, most of which are not suitable at this time for Western readers. However, it is interesting to note that many of them also require reciting the Dharani 21 times, sometimes 108 times or even 1080 times. The text then lists the 42 different Hands of Assistance for the resolving of specific problems and realizing goals and desires. These Hands are aspects of Bodhisattva power. According to tradition, each of the 42 Hands are recited with a corresponding phrase in the mantra, but not necessarily with a one-to-one correlation. Overlapping occurs as some of the Hands share the same phrase. Some translators use the word *Mudra* (sacred gesture) for Hand. Mantras for many of these Hands are included in Chapter 22.]

The Forty-Two Hands

An eighth-century translation by Amoghavajra lists 40 of these 42 Hands/Mudras in this sutra. Included here are illustrations for each Hand as drawn from traditional paintings. Additional descriptions of the Mudra gestures are provided where available.

1. For wealth and gems, perform the *cintamani mudra* of hand holding the wish fulfilling jewel (as-you-will pearl hand).

2. For freedom from worry, perform the *pasa mudra* with hand holding lariat rope (lasso hand).

3. For freedom from abdominal diseases, perform the *patra mudra* with hand holding a jewelled bowl.

4. To subdue ghosts and evil spirits, perform the *khadra mudra* with hand holding a sword (jeweled sword hand).

5. To subdue demons, perform the three-pointed *vajra mudra*.

107

6. To overcome enemies, perform the one-pronged *vajra mudra*. (*Index finger extended, other three fingers joined and bent inwards, thumb touching outside of middle finger near nail, done with both hands.*)

7. For release from fear and worry, make the *abhaya mudra* for fearlessness. (*Left hand on left thigh, right hand at heart facing outward, thumb and index finger spread, other three fingers joined.*)

8. For eyesight, perform the *suryamani mudra* of holding the sun disc with a crow inside of it (sun essence mani hand).

9. To remain calm, perform the *candramani mudra* of holding the moon disc with a tree and a rabbit inside of it.

10. To obtain a good career, perform the *dhanur mudra* of holding a jewelled bow.

11. To make good friends, perform the *bana mudra* of holding a jewelled arrow.

12. To be healed of sickness, perform the *willow branch mudra*.

13. To remove karmic obstacles, perform the *camari mudra* of holding a white whisk or brush.

14. For family harmony, perform the *kalasa mudra* of holding a water vase.

15. To keep away wild animals, perform the *bohai mudra* of holding a shield.

16. For avoiding legal problems, use the *parasu mudra* of holding an axe.

17. For good servants, perform the *jade-bracelet mudra*.

18. To obtain merit and virtues, perform the *pundarika mudra* of holding a white lotus.

19. To be reborn in the Pure Lands, use the *utpala mudra* of holding a blue lotus.

20. For attaining great wisdom, perform the *darpana mudra* of holding a jewelled mirror.

21. To meet the buddhas of the ten directions, make the *purple lotus mudra*.

22. For finding treasure in the ground, perform the *jewel chest mudra*.

23. To achieve the Way of the Immortals, perform the *fivecolored- cloud mudra*.

24. For rebirth in Brahma heaven, perform the *kundi mudra* of a water bottle resting on the palm.

25. To be reborn in heavenly palaces, perform the *padma mudra* of holding a red lotus.

26. To avoid robbery, perform the *kunta mudra* of holding a jewelled javelin (halberd).

27. To summon good spirits, use the *sankha mudra* of holding a jewelled conch shell. *(Clasp your left thumb with the fingers of your right hand so the thumb is encircled by four fingers. Keep the fingers of the left hand straight. Touch the upper side of the right thumb to the upper side of the left index finger. Hold the mudra in front of your heart.)*

28. To summon and command spirits, perform the *munda mudra* of the skull (skull staff)

29. To call the buddhas of the ten directions to give predictions, make the *aksamala mudra* of holding prayer beads.

30. To have a great speaking voice and musicality, perform the *ghanta mudra* of holding the bell.

31. For eloquence, use the *jewelled-seal mudra*.

32. For protection by nature's devas and dragon kings, perform the *ankusa mudra* of holding an iron hook.

33. To protect all beings with compassion, perform the *danda mudra* of holding a monk's tin staff.

34. To have all beings be loving and respectful, use the *jali mudra* of your palms joined in prayer.

35. To be with buddhas in every life, perform the *transformation buddha mudra*.

36. To be reborn in buddha palaces and never from a physical womb, perform the *transformation-palace mudra*.

37. For great wisdom and learning, use the *sutra mudra* of holding the jewelled sutra.

38. To achieve a non-retreating, awakening mind until one is enlightened, perform the *cakravarticakra mudra* of holding a gold wheel.

39. For the buddhas of the ten directions to rub you on the crown to confer predictions, use the *Usnisa Buddha mudra* of Buddha on the Crown.

40. For bountiful crops, perform the *amalaka mudra* of holding a cluster of grapes.

116

The sutra traditionally has these two additional Hands not given by Amoghavajra:

41. To alleviate hunger and thirst of all living creatures, perform the *pouring-sweet-dew mudra*.

42. To subdue demons in the threethousand worlds, perform the *uniting-and-holding-the-thousandarms mudra*.

(Right hand resting on left, palms upward.)

Next, the Sunlight Bodhisattva and Moonlight Bodhisattva each give a mantra for the protection of those who recite the Dharani. They are, respectively:

1. ***Namo Buddha Kunami, Namo Dharma Mahedi, Nama Sangha Dayeni, Dibubi Satva, Yam Namo***

and

2. ***Sumdidi Tushuteza Ehjamidi Wudutza, Sunkitza, Bwolaidi, Yemijatzu Wudutza, Kaladitza, Kimwotza svaha***

The sutra declares that reciting this mantra erases all offenses, protects one from demons and prevents natural disasters. Westerners tend to be unaware of the demonic source of many of the world's problems. Demons can have a powerful influence on people and events.

The Buddha then tells Ananda to accept and hold the Dharani with a pure heart, disseminate it widely, and never allow it to be lost or to become extinct. It can cure all disease and can even cause a withered tree to renew itself and grow fruit. The power of this Dharani is inconceivable. If one has not planted good deeds in the past, one cannot even hear its name, let alone find it. Those who doubt or slander the Dharani cannot receive its benefits.

After hearing the Buddha praise the Dharani, the entire enormous assembly accepted the teaching and began practicing it.

* * *

Note on the Code of Conduct

Mastery of sexual energy takes time and diligence. We are intended to become its master, not its slave. Most spiritual wisdom, both ancient and modern, recognizes the need for preserving this sacred energy rather than recklessly squandering it. This does not necessarily mean abstinence, but rather treating it with honor and respect with a spiritually compatible spouse. I have given only a few examples of the misuse of this energy—the list is much longer. In the 20th century, the pendulum swung from sexual repression to the opposite extreme of self-indulgent promiscuity. Hopefully, it will now swing back to a more balanced middle ground.

The correct use of these energies is related to the positive and negative polarities of the chakras when they come together in sexual union. Elizabeth Haich's *Sexual Energy and Yoga* covers converting this energy to creative, spiritual energy in the higher nerve centers. Unfortunately, this book is out of print. Another good book is *Joy of No Sex* by Swami Bhaktipada, who says, "There is no victory more glorious than mastery of our own mind and senses.

Until we control the body and mind, we are subject to the slavery of cruel taskmasters."

Controlling our physical appetites is a lifelong project just like controlling our thoughts and feelings. If we remember the axiom, "Where attention goes, there energy flows," it can be our key to mastery of ourselves in all areas of life. When we guard the mind and choose to keep our attention away from the stimulating material that's constantly purveyed in the media, the job is much easier. To control the body, we must control the mind and develop the habit of instantly transferring thought to another area, perhaps with an inspirational or funny book, magazine or movie. Diverting this energy into a hobby or any of the arts, like writing poetry or sketching, can bring unexpected creative rewards.

Trying to achieve self-control in any sphere of life by sheer force of will power is unrealistic for most of us. "What we resist persists." Fortunately, Kuan Yin taught in the sutra that one of the innumerable benefits of sincere, regular recitation of The Great Compassion Mantra is achieving right use and mastery of sexual energies and release from sexual addictions.

CHAPTER 15 ~ **The Great Compassion Dharani Mantra (*Da Bei Zhou*) with Pronunciation Guide**

The original Sanskrit text of this mantra has been lost. This version is how the Chinese pronounced the Sanskrit in an early north-Indian copy. For example, "maha" became "mohe," "buddha" became "pu'sa," etc. It is comparable to how English peoples have anglicized foreign words, like Peking for Beijing, and so forth. Current Sanskrit versions are approximations derived from Chinese transliterations.

In researching this book, I found many variations in the spelling and pronunciation of these syllables and eventually relinquished my belief that there is only one correct way to recite them. Don't be surprised if you find it spelled and spoken differently on recordings on the Internet. A friend of mine has terrible Chinese pronunciation, and when she is reciting the mantras, her clairvoyant husband sometimes sees Kuan Yin smiling in amusement!

As with any prayer or mantra, our pronunciation is not as important as our sincerity and devotion, which connect us to the sponsoring saint or celestial being who empowers that mantra or prayer. We also connect with the energy of everyone currently giving the mantra and tie into the energy of all the times the mantra has ever been given through the ages—its *morphic field*. Thus we are tying into the power of a vast momentum of energy as well as adding to it. Our own vows merge with those of Kuan Yin for this mantra.

Some Chinese books have eighty-four illustrations that go with the lines of this mantra. They represent eighty-four manifestations of Kuan Yin.

Here is a review of the requirements for obtaining the promised results of this Dharani:

> • Keep the code of conduct given in the previous chapter at all times. Repent for all past offenses and forsake greed, anger, ignorance, untoward desires, lust and harsh speech. Develop compassion for all life—human, animal and plant, with no partaking of meat, alcohol or drugs.

• Sincerely recite the Ten Vows given in the previous chapter and also found in Chapter 21.

• Respectfully recite the names of Kuan Yin and her teacher, the Dhyani Buddha Amitabha, for example: *Namo Kuan Shih Yin* and *Om Amitabha Hri.* These are sometimes done three or nine times each.

• Preferably recite this mantra at least five times daily. This takes less than 15 minutes, much less as you get faster. Once a day is fine if you don't have 15 minutes. Many people do it 21 times a day or even 108 times daily. Repetition accumulates and multiplies the positive results of a mantra.

• To avoid mindless mechanical repetition, keep your awareness focused in your heart and on Kuan Yin while reciting. Activate the mantra with a feeling like faith, love, gratitude or devotion.

• Be consistent. Daily practice is the key to obtaining the spiritual and material rewards promised in the sutra.

The Great Compassionate Dharani Mantra

1. Namo he la da nwo duo la ye ye
 [NAH-mwoh HE(R) lah dah NWOH dwoh LAH yeh yeh]*

2. Namo a li ye
 [NAH-mwoh AH lee YEH]

3. Po lu jie di shau bo la ye
 [PWOH loo je-EH dee SHOH bwoh LA yeh]

4. Pu ti sa duo pe ye
 [POO tee SHAH dwoh peh YEH]

5. Mo he sa duo pe ye
 [MWOH ho SHAH dwoh peh YEH]

6. Mo he jia lu ni jia ye
   [MWOH ho je-AH loo nee je-AH YEH]

7. Nan
   [Nun]

8. Sa pan la fa ye
   [SAH pun lah FAH yeh]

9. Swo da nwo da xie
   [SHWOH dah nwoh DAH see-EH]

10. Namo xi ji li duo yi meng a li ye
    [NAH-moh SEE jee lee dwoh YEE mung AH-lee yeh]

11. Pe lu ji di shi fwo la leng tuo pe
    [PE(R) loo JEE dee shu(r) fwoh la LUNG twoh poh]

12. Namo nuo la jin chi(r)
    [NAH-mwoh nwoh lah JIN-juh]

13. Xi li mo he pan duo sa mie
    [SEE lee mwoh-ho PUN dwoh SHAH me-EH]

14. Sa pe e tuo dou shu peng
    [SHAH pe(r) AH twoh DOH shoo pung]

15. A shi yun
    [AH shu(r) yoon]

16. Sa pe sa duo, namo pe sa duo, namo pe jie
    [SHAH pe(r) SHAH dwoh, NAH-mwoh pe(r) SHAH dwoh, NAH-mwoh pe(r) che-EH]

17. Mo fa te duo
    [Mwoh-FAH teh DOH]

18. Dah zhi tuo
    [DAH juh twoh]

19. Nan e pu lu xi
    [NUN e(r) poo LOO see]

20. Lu jia di
    [LOO je-AH dee]

21. Jia la di
    [Je-AH lah DEE]

22. Yi xi li
    [YEE see lee]

23. Mo he pu ti sa duo
    [MWOH ho POO tee SAH dwoh]

24. Sa pe sa pe
    [SHAH pe(r) SHAH po]

25. Mo la mo la
    [MWOH lah MWOH lah]

26. Mo xi mo xi li tuo yun
    [MWOH see MWOH see LEE twoh YOON]

27. Jyu lu jyu lu jie meng
    [Je-OO loo Je-OO loo Je-YEH mung]

28. Du lu du lu fa she ye di
    [DOO loo DOO loo, FAH she(r) yeh DEE]

29. Mo he fa she ye di
    [MWOH ho FAH she(r) yeh DEE]

30. Tuo la tuo la
    [DWOH lah DWOH lah]

31. Di li ni
    [DEE lee nee]

32. Shi fwo la ye
    [SHE(R)-fwoh lah YEH]

33. Je la je la
    [JEH lah JEH lah]

34. Mo mo fa mo la
    [MWOH mwoh FAH mwoh LAH]

35. Mu di li
    [MOO dee lee]

36. Yi xi yi xi
    [YEE see YEE see]

37. Shi nwo shi nwo
    [SHE(R) nwoh SHE(R) nwoh]

38. A la shen fwo la she li
    [AH lah SHUN fwoh LAH she(r) LEE]

39. Fa sha fa shen
    [Fah SHAH fah SHUN]

40. Fwo la she ye
    [FWOH lah she(r) YEH]

41. Hu lu hu lu mo la
    [HOO loo HOO loo MWOH lah]

42. Hu lu hu lu xi li
    [HOO loo HOO loo SEE lee]

43. Suo la, suo la
    [SHOH lah, SHOH lah]

44. Xi li, xi li
    [SEE lee, SEE lee]

45. Su lu, su lu
    [SHOO loo, SHOO loo]

46. Pu ti ye, pu ti ye
    [Poo TEE yeh, poo TEE yeh]

47. Pu tuo ye, pu tuo ye
    [Poo TWOH yeh, poo TWOH yeh]

48. Mi di li ye
    [MEE dee lee YEH]

49. Nwo la jin chr
    [NWOH lah JIN-juh]

50. Di li shai ni nwoh
    [DEE lee SHY nee nwoh]

51. Po ye mo nwo
    [POH yeh mwoh NWOH]

52. Sa po ho
    [SHO paw ho]

53. Xi two ye
    [SEE twoh yeh]

54. Sa po ho
    [SHO paw ho]

55. Mo he xi two ye
    [MWOH ho SEE twoh YEH]

56. Sa po ho
    [SHO paw ho]

57. Xi tuo yu yi
    [SEE twoh yoo YEE]

58. Shi pan la ye
    [SHE(R) pun lah YEH]

59. Sa po ho
    [SHO paw ho]

60. Nwo la jin chr
    [NWOH lah JIN-juh]

61. Sa po ho
    [SHO paw ho]

62. Mo la nwo la
    [MWOH lah NWOH lah]

63. Sa po ho
    [SHO paw ho]

64. Xi lu seng a mu jie ye
    [SEE loo SUNG ah MOO ch-yeh YEH]

65. Sa po ho
    [SHO paw ho]

66. Sa po mo he e xi tuo ye
    [SHO paw MWOH ho e(r) SEE twoh YEH]

67. Sa po ho
    [SHO paw ho]

68. Je ji la, e xi tuo ye
    [JEH jee lah, e(r) SEE twoh YEH]

69. Sa po ho
    [SHO paw ho]

70. Bwo tuo mo jie xi tuo ye
    [BWOH twoh MWOH je-EH SEE twoh YEH]

71. Sa po ho
    [SHO paw ho]

72. Nwo la jin chr pan jie la ye
    [NWOH la JIN-jer PUN je-EH lah YEH]

73. Sa po ho
    [SHO paw ho]

74. Mo pe li sheng jie la ye
    [MWOH peh LEE shung je-EH lah YEH]

75. Sa po ho
    [SHO paw ho]

76. Namo he la da nwo duo la ye ye
    [NAH-moh HEH lah dah NWOH dwoh LAH yeh yeh]

77. Namo a li ye
    [NAH-mwoh AH lee yeh]

78. Pe lu jie di
    [PEH loo je-EH dee]

79. Shau pan la ye
    [SHOH pun LAH yeh]

80. Sa po ho
    [SHO paw ho]

81. Nan xi dian du
    [NUN see de-UN doo]1

82. Man duo la
    [MUN dwoh LAH]

83. Pa tuo ye
    [BAH twoh YEH]

84. Sa po ho
    [SHO paw ho]

*The (r) shown in parentheses is not strongly pronounced, but used as a guide to pronounce the preceding vowel as if the letter were there. Thus he(r) and shu(r) are pronounced somewhat as "her" and "shur" with almost no emphasis on the "r" sound.

** Capitalized syllables are stressed.

CHAPTER 16 ~ **The Great Compassion Dharani Mantra in Sanskrit with Translation**

I learned this version and pronunciation from an old Chinese monk who recommended chanting it with the prayer mudra (palms joined) until at least line ten or for the entire dharani. This version is probably easier for English-speaking people to memorize, so it can be done anywhere. It looks like Pali, but the monk called it Sanskrit, so I'm calling it that. It is customary to make the dedication at the end rather than at the beginning.

Just say out loud that you dedicate this chanting for whatever or whomever you wish. Include your own needs as well as those of your family and friends, and for world situations. For Kuan Yin there are no limits, so always "maximize your calls" to include all people suffering under similar conditions.

Constancy with this mantra is said to remove fear, greed, ignorance, hatred, jealousy, anger and other negative feelings and addictions. Repetition multiplies the energy like winding more coils around a magnet or when swirling a lasso before releasing it. Do the same number of repetitions daily and stick to a schedule.

MAHA KARUNIKA CITTA DHARANI
[Ma-HA kah-roo-NIK-ah CHI-tah DHAH-rah-nee]

1. Namo ratnatrayaya
   [NAH-moh RUT-nah-trah-YAH-yah]

2. Nama arya Avalokitesvaraya
   [Nah-MAH AH-ree-yah AH-vah-loh-KEET-es-vah-RAH-yah]

3. Bodhisattvaya, Mahasattvaya, Mahakarunikaya
   [BU-dee-sut-VAH-ya, ma-HA-sut-VAH-ya, ma-HA-KAR-roo-NEE-KY-ah]

4. OM, sarva rabhaye sudhanadasya
   [Ohm, sahr-VAH rub-HA-yeh sud-DUN-nah-DUH-see-ya]

129

5. Nama skritvanimam
   [NAH-mah SKRIT-vahn-ee-MUM]

6. Arya Avalokitesvara ramdhava
   [AH-ree-ya AH-vah-loh-keet-es-VAH-rah RUM-dah-vah]

7. Namo narakindi HRIH Mahavadasvame
   [NAH-moh nah-rah-KIN-dee hree ma-HA-vah-das-VAH-may]

8. Sarva arthatosubham ajeyum
   [Sahr-VAH ar-tuh-too-ZOO-bahm ah-JAY-um]

9. Sarvasatya nama vasatya namo vaka mavitato
   [Sahr-VAH-SUT-ee-ya, nah-MAH vah-SUT-ya, NAH-moh VAH-kah mah-vee-DUT-too]

10. Tadyatha
    [TUD-ee-ah-tah]

11. Om avaloki lokate karate e HRIH Maha-Bodhisattva
    [Ohm ah-vah-LOH-kee loh-KAH-tay kah-RAH-tay ay hree ma-HA-BU-dee-SUT-vah]

12. Sarva sarva
    [SAHR-vah SAHR-vah]

13. Mala mala
    [Mah-LAH mah-LAH]

14. Mahi Mahi ridhayum
    [MAH-hee MAH-hee rid-ee-DY-um]

15. Kuru Kuru Karmam
    [Koo-ROO koo-ROO KAR-mum]

16. Dhuru dhuru
    [Doo-ROO doo-ROO]

17. Vijayate Mahavijayate
    [Vih-jee-YAH-tay mah-HA-vih-jee-YAH-tay]

18. Dhara dhara dhrini
    [Dah-RAH da-RAH dih-rih-NEE]

19. Svaraya cala cala
    [Shvah-RY-yah cha-LA cha-LA]

20. Mama vimala muktele
    [Ma-MA VIM-ah-lah MOOK-teh-leh]

21. Ehi-ehi sina sina
    [AY-hee AY-hee sin-NAH sin-NAH]

22. Arsam prachali
    [Ar-ZUM PRAH-chah-lee]

23. Visva visvam prasaya
    [Vis-VAH vis-VUM PRAH-sah-yah]

24. Hulu hulu mara
    [Hoo-LOO hoo-LOO mah-RAH]

25. Hulu hulu HRIH
    [Hoo-LOO hoo-LOO hree]

26. Sara sara, siri siri, suru suru
    [Sah-RAH sah-RAH, sih-REE sih-REE, soo-ROO soo-ROO]

27. Bodhiya bodhiya, bodhaya bodhaya!
    [Bu-dee-YAH bu-dee-YAH, bu-dy-AH bu-dy-AH!]

28. Maitreya narakindi dharishinina bhayamana svaha
    [May-tree-YAH nah-rah-KIN-dee da-ris-sin-in-AH bah-yah-MAH-nah shvah-HA]

29. Siddhaya svaha
    [Sid-DY-yah shvah-HA]

30. Maha siddhaya svaha
    [Ma-HA sid-DY-ah shvah-HA]

31. Siddhayoge svaraya svaha
    [Sid-ha-YOH-gay shva-RY-ah shvah-HA]

32. Narakindi svaha
    [Nah-rah-KIN-dee shvah-HA]

33. Maranara svaha
    [MA-rah NAH-rah shvah-HA]

34. Sri simha-mukaya svaha
    [Sree SIM-ha-mook-KAY-ya shvah-HA]

35. Sarva Maha asiddhaya svaha
    [SAR-va ma-HA ah-sid-HY-ya shvah-HA]

36. Cakra asiddhaya svaha
    [CHUK-rah ah-sid-DY-ya shvah-HA]

37. Padma kastaya svaha
    [PUD-ma kus-TY-ah shvah-HA]

38. Narakindi vagalaya svaha
    [Nah-rah-KIN-dee vuh-guh-LY-ya shvah-HA]

39. Mavari sankharaya svaha
    [Ma-vah-REE sunk-har-RY-ya shvah-HA]

40. Nama ratnatrayaya
    [Nah-MAH RUT-nah-tray-YAH-ya]

41. Namo arya Avalokitesvaraya svaha
    [Nah-MO AH-ree-yah AH-vah-loh-KEET-es-vah-RAH-yah shvah-HA]

42. Om sidhyantu mantra padaya svaha
    [Ohm sid-AHN-too MUN-trah pud-DY-ah shvah-HA]

Approximate Translation of the Sanskrit Great Compassion Dharani Mantra

It is not necessary to focus on the meaning of the mantra, as the power comes from the sounds, the devotion and from the Bodhisattva, rather than from an intellectual understanding. Preoccupation with meaning can distract and get in the way of achieving the benefits. Still, we provide the translations here to give you a glimpse of its power and beauty.

I take refuge in the Three Treasures.
I take refuge in Avalokitesvara, the great Compassionate Bodhisattva,
    Mahasattva.

OM, to the one who springs beyond all fear!
Revering him, I enter the heart of the noble, divinely honored blue-necked
    Avalokitesvara.
This is culmination of all significance, purity, enabling victory for all beings
    and cleansing the path of beingness.

Therefore,
OM, the seer, the transcendent one,
HRIH! Mahabodhisattva!
All! All!
Soiled, soiled!
The earth, the earth.
It is the Heart
Perform, perform the work!
Hold on, hold on!

O great victorious one
Hold, hold,
I cling to the Creator
Move, move, my uncontaminated seal
Come, come,
Hear, hear,
Bliss arises within me
Speak, speak! Guidance!
Hulu Hulu Mala, Hulu Hulu HRIH!

Sara Sara, Siri Siri, Suru Suru,
Awaken, awaken! Have enlightenment, have enlightenment!

Compassionate blue-necked one!
Of courageous ones, to the blissful, hail!

To the triumphant one, hail!
To the great triumphant one, hail!
To the one with the attainment of all mastery, hail!
To the blue-necked one, hail!
To the boar-faced one, hail!
To the lion-headed one, hail!
To the weapon-wielding one, hail!
To the wheel-holding one, hail!
To the lotus-holding one, hail!
To the blue-necked, far-affecting one, hail!
To the magnanimous one in the beginning of this Dharani, hail!

I take refuge in the Three Treasures,
I take refuge in Avalokitesvara, hail!

Let this mantra swiftly succeed!
To this power mantra, hail!

[Based on the work of Dr. Suzuki]

CHAPTER 17 ~ **What Is the Heart Sutra?**

Written in the first century CE, the Heart Sutra, with only fourteen Sanskrit verses, is the shortest of the thirty-eight *Prajnaparamita* (Perfection of Wisdom) Sutras. It was translated into Chinese by master translator Kumarajiva late in the third century. In the text, Avalokitesvara (Kuan Yin) addresses the devotee, Sariputra, giving him a very succinct distillation of enlightened awareness and transcendent wisdom. The sutra has hidden levels of meaning and ends with a mantra containing the essence of the teaching. The entire sutra, known as the Ultimate Mantra, is usually chanted in Chinese. The concluding mantra when recited on its own may be done in either Chinese, Sanskrit or Pali. The sutra may be translated into English as follows [with my notes in brackets]:

The Heart of the Perfection of Wisdom Sutra

The Bodhisattva Avalokitesvara [Kuan Shih Yin], engaged in the deep practice of Perfected Wisdom, looked down and beheld that all five Skandas [form, sensation, perception impulses and consciousness] were empty, and thereby was enabled to transcend all sufferings, saying:

"Sariputra, here at this level, form differs not from emptiness and emptiness differs not from form. Form is emptiness and emptiness is form. This is also true for sensation, perception, mental impulses and consciousness.

"O Sariputra, these are all marked with emptiness, neither arising nor ceasing, neither defiled nor immaculate, neither increasing nor diminishing.

"Thus, in emptiness there is no form, sensation, perception, impulses, nor consciousness; no eye, ear, nose, tongue, body, nor mind; no form, sound, smell, taste, touch, nor mental object; no visual elements and so on [for the other senses] until we come to no mental-awareness elements.

"There is neither ignorance nor ending of ignorance, and so forth, until we come to there is no old age nor death, nor ending of old age and death.

"There is no suffering, no cause of suffering, neither ceasing of suffering, nor Path. "There is no wisdom; no attainment nor non-attainment. Because there is nothing to be attained, the Bodhisattvas relying on this Prajna Paramita [Perfection of Wisdom] dwell in it and are without thought impediments.

"Being free of thought impediments, they are free from fear and beyond error. They have overcome upsets, the confusion of delusion, and so, ultimately they attain Nirvana.

"All the Buddhas of past, present and future, by relying on this profound Prajna Paramita, achieve Ultimate Enlightenment.

"Thus know this Prajna Paramita as the great Sacred Incantation [mantra], the incantation of great illumination, the ultimate and unequalled incantation that truly mitigates all suffering unfailingly.

"Therefore utter this mantra of the Perfection of Wisdom saying, 'Gate gate paragate parasamgate Bodhi svaha!'"

[This translates to "Gone, gone, gone beyond, gone completely beyond, Enlightenment! hail!" The word svaha is a term of blessing, ratification and joyful exclamation, as in "so be it!" that is difficult to translate into English].

In this section, we are given a direct and simple translation of the Heart Sutra. Following in the next chapter, Shanti Hee gives us her more elaborate mystical interpretation along with the Chinese characters and English phonetics.

Commentary on the Sutra

To traditional Buddhism, this sutra initially appears horrifying as it seemingly negates all its basic tenets. Author John Blofeld maintains that this is to "shock the hearer into sudden apprehension" of the delusion of "a real and permanent ego" and to attain a direct experience of "emptiness," which is nonconceptual.

To the outer-worldly mind, the dialectical verses of this sutra may seem absurd and selfcontradictory. Like descriptions of Nirvana or Samadhi, it can only be comprehended by those who have already experienced them.

The verses can be penetrated by those who have a razor-sharp mind entrained with the heart to make the leap to an aha! experience of direct realization. It also requires mastery of meditation or deep contemplation.

Because it appears to say, "X is what X is not," it cannot be apprehended by logical reasoning. Its wisdom transcends our world of dualism. A few commentators have noted that some phrases do not mean what they say. Some have fallen into the trap of equating void or emptiness with nothingness. Likewise equating the unmanifest with nothing is also an error, especially now that we have scientific knowledge of the implicate order and the Zero Point Field and Source Field.

Some translations use the word "void" in place of "emptiness." But the void is not vacuity. His Holiness, the Dalai Lama, uses emptiness instead of void, as a better translation of the sutra, as void and The Great Void have different meanings. The Dalai Lama says that the emptiness referred to in this sutra is not referring to the absolute stratum of reality, but instead refers to phenomena, and that all phenomena has no permanent, independent, intrinsic existence of its own. It always comes to an end because it is a transitory collection of light and sound vibration. It does not imply non-existence.

Tibetan lamas considered The Great Void to be undifferentiated Unity. In deep meditation they access a direct experience of Infinity and Oneness in a higher dimensional octave where all definitions and concepts of our three-dimensional world no longer apply.

In his classic book, W*holeness and the Implicate Order*, physicist David Bohm speaks of the immeasurable primary essence of reality as it is enfolded within the implicate order. In his words, we live in the explicate order—"the perceptible aspect of the world coming out of a more comprehensive implicate order in which all aspects ultimately merge in an indefinable and immeasurable holomovement." He agrees with the ancients who maintain that when what is measurable is identified with the very essence of reality, that is illusion.

The implicate order is considered by some to be The Great Void—the plane or dimension from which all phenomena arises and returns. It is the Source of energy and consciousness, the Source Field. Others consider the Void to be even beyond that, as a super-spiritual realm incomprehensible to both our limited five senses and our intellect.

It has also been postulated that The Great Void contains the Zero Point Field, the immense quantum sea of latent energy created by the continual transfer of energy and information between subatomic, virtual particles. This field fills the entire universe, including all so-called empty space that is now known to be full of energy, electrons, etc.

Emptiness and the unmanifest can be equated with no–thing–ness, which is quite different from nothingness. The seeming negations in this text actually lead to ultimate reality, which is beyond all labels, beyond all duality.

Two millennia ago, when the Heart Sutra was given as part of the esoteric wisdom for advanced spiritual students, it was not intended for the dull-minded or uninformed. Perhaps now the time has come to utilize our so-called advanced scientific knowledge, wedded to a deep heart connection, as a bridge to mystical wisdom and thereby gain transcendent insights far beyond the limitations of the intellect.

The *Prajnaparamita* texts came after the basic teachings had already been given. They presupposed an advanced spirituality and a knowledge of the earlier scriptures that were generally known at that time.

Avalokitesvara, also known as the Bestower of Mantras, reveals this sutra as the ultimate mantra to alleviate all suffering and to remove all evil. According to ancient traditions, there is nothing that mantras cannot achieve when done correctly. They were not composed arbitrarily, but came from higher beings, contain their essence and vibration, and create a connection to them. Because they encode energy in the form of sound frequencies, vocalizing the syllables aloud is important, even if whispered.

CHAPTER 18 ~ **The Heart Sutra of Kuan Yin & Mystical Meaning**

by Shanti Hee

波羅蜜多心経

When Shanti Hee came to visit us in Montana, she copied the Chinese characters (as shown) from a painting at Christine Meiner's house, then spent the entire night writing out her extended, interpretive meanings and the Chinese transliterations. I have added the pronunciation guides in brackets.

観自在菩薩

1. Guan zi zai P'u Sa
[GWUN* juh ZY Poo Sah]
> In the perfected state of wisdom, the Bodhisattva resides at the point of absolute truth, deep inner knowing, and complete stillness of intelligent being—a Pure Spirit viewer from the formless plane through the transcendental entrance point in the heart's core essence [Zero Point], observing the outer universe as being Pure Spirit.

行深

2. Xing shen
[SING shun]
> Perfected practice resulting in the deep realization of the inner spiritual truth of our existence as being purely energies of Spirit.

般若

3. Ban jou
   [BUN joh]
   Is likened to

波 羅 蜜 多 時

4. Bo lou mi duo shi
   *[BWAW law ME du-AW shu(r)**]*
   The transcendent, spiritual sight at the point of convergence with the Source at the heart's inner core beyond time and space [Zero Point], seeing the infinite, unified, living energy-field of unmanifest potentialities as the Source from which all physical manifestations arise and return.

照見

5. Zhao jian
   [Jao je-EN]
   In a state of profound realization of illumination,

五蘊皆空

6. Wu yun jie kong
   [Wu yin je-EH kong]

Through the spiritual sight at the transcendent point of universal unity in the center of the heart [Zero Point], is the realization that only pure, living-energy frequencies are the true nature of all physical manifestation observable by the five senses.

度一切苦厄

7. Du yi qie ku e
[Du yee chi-EH koo UH]
This Realization of the Beyond in the heart-core convergence point with the formless liberates and frees you from afflictions and suffering. One crosses into the beyond — beyond physical, sensory perception and suffering.

舍利子

8. Shi li zi
[Su(r) LEE juh]
In this state of Realization, pure Spirit imprints in our physical-body cells an RNA/DNA crystallization of that pure Consciousness.

色不異空

9. Se bu yi kong
[Su(r) bu YEE kong]

Visible physical form is not different from the pure energy inherent in the unmanifest formlessness of pure space.

空不異色

10. Kong bu yi se
[Kong bu YEE su(r)]
> The pure Zero-Point Field (Source Field) of formless energy, invisible to physical sight, is no different from the energy manifesting in physical form.

色即是空

11. Se ji shi kong
[Su(r) juh shu(r) kong]
> Visible physical forms embody the pure energy from the formless domain and are created from the nothingness [unmanifest] state out of the energy, consciousness and love of the formless plane.

空即是色

12. Kong ji shi se
[Kong juh shu(r) su(r)]
> Pure energy via pure Consciousness manifests as pure, visible form in pure space in the nexus at the heart-core [Zero Point]. Form and nonform co-exist and are transformable from one to the other at this [Zero-Point] convergence.

受想行識

13. Shou xiang xing shi
 [SHOW si-UNG sing shu(r)]
   This is also true for our senses, perceptions, impulses and conscious thoughts.

亦復如是

14. Yi fu ru shi
 [YEE fu roo shu(r)]
   In truth, they are pure energy expressions in space.

舍利子

15. She li zi
 [Su(r) LEE juh]
   In this state of apparent nothingness at the heart-core nexus, pure Consciousness of pure energy crystallizes as our physical form.

是諸法空相

16. Shi zhu fa kong xiang
 [Su(r) JU fah kong si-ung]
   Physical forms are illusions created from the pure, infinite energy-field (Source Field) by the various individual thoughtform projections.

143

不生

17. Bu sheng
[Bu SHUNG]
This energy field has no beginning nor birth.

不滅

18. Bu mie
[Bu me-EH]
It has no end, nor can it be destroyed.

不垢

19. Bu gou
[Bu goh]
As pure energy it is neither defiled nor soiled.

不淨

20. Bu jing
[Bu jing]
Yet it is not clean or immaculate.

不增不減

21. Bu zeng, bu jian
[Bu jung bu je-EN]
It is not increasing nor decreasing.

是故空中無色

22. Shi gu kong zhong wu se
[Shu(r) gu kong jong wu su(r)]
It is from this state of the apparent nothingness of infinite potential, the consciousness of the living, unified convergence at the heart-core [Zero-Point] that existence manifests.

無受想行識

23. Wu shou xiang xing shi
[Wu SHOW si-UNG sing shu(r)]
There is no true separation between various, different forms. There is only one unified field of sensation, perception, impulse and consciousness of all-being, all-knowing, all-seeing and all-love.

無眼耳鼻舌身意

24. Wu yan er bi shi shen yi
[Wu YUN-ar bee shu(r) SHEN yee]

In the pure Spirit-Beingness at the living, unified, universal convergence at our heart-core [Zero Point], exists our formless, inner, spiritual senses of sight, hearing, smell, taste and feeling, and also the transcendent awareness of the one, pure Consciousness of the unified field of pure energy expressed in our visible form.

無色声香味触法

25. Wu se sheng xiang wei chu fa
[Wu su(r) sheng si-UNG way CHOO fah]
As pure spirit in this living, unified convergence-portal in the heart, we all have one unified vision. We all have unified hearing of the one-heart tone, smelling of the one-heart fragrance, feeling of the one-body of our pure-heart, and realizing of the one, same consciousness of our inner Spirit - the pure expression of Love.

無限界

26. Wu yan jie
[Wu yun je-EH]
At this point of our heart-core, our pure Beingness is not attached to the reactions of outer sight, nor to the outer mental and physical worlds.

乃至無意識界

27. Nai zhi wu yi shi jie
[NAY juh wu yee shu(r) je-EH]

Likewise, within this truth in our heart-core, the essence of our true Beingness is not attached to the outer-worldly conditioning or programming of the outer consciousness of matter thought-forms.

無無明

28. Wu wu ming
[Wu wu ming]

In the state of this connection with Spirit in the heart [Zero-Point], we never lose our immense, one, true Inner Light.

亦無無明尽

29. Yi wu wu ming, jin
[Yee wu wu MING jin]

Likewise, in this state we are never lost in the outer, fragmented thoughtforms of the finite matter-world's conditioning that is ultimately unreal.

乃至無老死

30. Nai zhi, wu lao shi
[Nay juh, wu LAO su(r)]

In this state at the heart connection with our eternal, pure, living Beingness [Zero Point], there is no perception of death.

亦無老死盡

31. Yi wu, lao shi jin
[Yee wu, LAO su(r) JIN]

Likewise, once we have merged completely with this state of heart-core connection with our true-essence Being of pure Light/Energy/Consciousness, there will be no more of the reincarnation cycle of karma and rebirth into our physical form.

無苦集滅道

32. Wu ku ji mie dao
[WU ku juh me-EH dao]

In this state of pure Beingness in our heart-core essence at the convergence, there can be no perception of suffering and no projection of fragmented, separate thoughtforms. There is no destructiveness in the absolute, perfect Wisdom of our heart-core Spirit-Being as pure Light Energy.

無智亦無得

33. Wu zhi yi wu de
[WU juh yee WU de(r)]

In the pure Beingness at the heart's center, we access the unified field of Divine Knowledge, the awareness of the connection of the Divine within us to the One Source of All, and the awareness of our equality in this Divine Love.

以無所得故

34. Yi wu suo de gu
    [Yee wu su-oh de(r) gu]
    In our Beingness as Pure Spirit in our heart-core, there is no effort and no need to strive for attainment, for we are centered in the heart of Love.

菩提薩埵依

35. Pu ti sa duo yi
    [POO tee SAH dwoh yee]
    The Bodhisattva is in her natural state of pure Beingness with no attachments.

般若波羅蜜多

36. Ban jou bo luo mi duo
    [BUN joh bwaw law ME dwaw]
    Her perceptions and manifest physicality are in accordance with the perfect Wisdom of this state and in perfect peace and harmony with the physical plane of existence.

故 心無罣礙

37. Gu xin, wu gua ai
[Gu SIN, wu gu-ah AY]
There she has no mental impediments nor defilements in her mind.

無罣礙故無有恐怖

38. Wu gua ai, gu wu you kong bu
[Wu gu-ah-AY, gu wu YOH kong bu]
In the absence of impediments is the absence of fear.

遠離顛倒無想

39. Yuan li dian dao, meng xiang
[Yu-en lee de-EN dao, mung si-ung]
Far beyond in pure Beingness, there is no inverted and illusory thought and no attachment to outer material forms. It is beyond the illusory forms of the physical.

究竟涅槃

40. Jiu jing nie pan
[Je-OO jing nee-EH pun]
In the pure bliss of Nirvana,

三世諸仏依

41. San shi zhu fo yi
 [SUN shuh JU fah yee]
   All fully realized Buddhas of the three worlds—past, present,
   and future,

般若波羅蜜多

42. Ban jou bo luo mi duo
 [Bun joh baw law ME du-aw]
   In the pure Beingness at their [Zero-Point] heart-core, are in their
   natural, true state with absolute Wisdom of living truth.

故 得阿耨

43. Gu de e nou
 [Gu de(r) AH no]
   Therefore effortlessly and by grace,

多羅三藐三菩提

44. Duo luo, san miao, san pu ti
 [Dwaw law, SUN miao, SUN poo tee]

Attain this natural, pure, spiritual state of perfect wisdom, transforming falsehood in the three worlds of past, present, and future.

故知般若波羅蜜多

45. Gu zhi, ban jou bo luo mi duo
 [Gu juh, BUN joh bwaw law ME dwaw]
　　Therefore, this Heart Sutra of Perfect Wisdom of Truth

是大神呪 是大明呪

46. Shi da shen zhou, shi da ming zhou
 [Shu(r) DAH shen jo, shu(r) DAH ming jo]
　　Is a great spiritual mantra, a mantra of great insight, having the power to evoke spiritual awakening.

是無上呪 是無等等呪

47. Shi wu shang zhou, shi wu deng deng shou
 [Shu(r) WU shung joh, shu(r) wu dung-dung joh]
　　This is an unsurpassed, supreme mantra—an unequalled, sacred mantra

能除一切苦

48. Neng chu, yi qui ku
[NUNG choo, yee chi-EH ku]
That calms the mind and removes all suffering.

真実不嘘

49. Zhen shi bu xu
[JUN shu(r) BU su(r)]
It reveals absolute spiritual truth without deception.

故説般若波羅蜜多呪

50. Gu shuo, ban jou, bo luo mi duo zhou
[GU shu-oh, BUN joh, bwaw law ME dwaw joh]
Therefore, when this Heart Sutra is spoken as a mantra,

即説呪曰

51. Ji shuo, zhou yue:
[Juh shu-oh, jo yu-EH]
You should also recite the following sacred words:

揭諦揭諦波羅揭諦

52. Jie di, jie di, bo luo jie di
[Je-EH dee, je-EH dee, bwaw law je-EH dee]
Gone, gone, gone Beyond.

波羅僧揭諦

53. Bo luo seng, jie di
[Bwaw law sung, je-EH dee]
Gone altogether Beyond.

菩提薩婆訶

54. Pu ti sa po he
[POO tee sah paw huh]
O what an awakening, Praise God!
Hail to all Bodhisattvas!

This final mantra (numbers 52 to 54) can also be given in the Pali form as:

Gate gate paragate parasamgate Bodhi svaha
[GUT-tay GUT-tay PAHrah GUT-tay pah-rahSUM GUT-tay BO-dee SHVAH-ha]

*Capitalized syllables are stressed.

**The (r) shown in parentheses is not strongly pronounced, but used as a guide to pronounce the preceding vowel as if the letter were there. Thus he(r) and shu(r) are pronounced somewhat as "her" and "shur" with almost no emphasis on the "r" sound.

The Heart Sutra

Traditional clerical script version of the Heart Sutra, courtesy of Andrew Owen. Chinese characters shown here read from up to down starting on the right. The version of the Heart Sutra in Chapter 18 includes a modern version of these Chinese characters arranged in the Western orientation of left to right.

CHAPTER 19 ~ **The Heart Sutra: A Pronunciation for English Readers**

It is best to recite the Heart Sutra while looking at the words in the previous chapter and also with your peripheral vision simultaneously taking in the Chinese characters and the mystical meaning. There is a saying "What the eye beholds the souls unfolds," and your soul will absorb the deeper nuances and spiritual energy of the characters and explanations.

This can be a bit confusing at first, so the following is a simple pronunciation guide to use occasionally until your eyes get used to quickly finding the pronunciation lines in the previous chapter, or until the pronunciations are memorized, by and large.

1. GWUN* juh ZY Poo Sah

2. SING shun

3. BUN joh

4. BWAW law ME du-AW shu(r)**

5. Jao je-EN

6. Wu yin je-EH Kong

7. Du yee chi-EH Koo UH.

8. Su(r) LEE juh

9. Su(r) bu YEE kong

10. Kong bu YEE su(r)

11. Su(r) juh shu(r) kong

12. Kong juh shu(r) su(r)

13. SHOW si-UNG sing shu(r)

14. YEE fu roo shu(r)

15. Su(r) LEE juh

16. Su(r) JU fah kong si-ung

17. Bu SHUNG

18. Bu me-EH

19. Bu goh

20. Bu jing

21. Bu jung bu je-EN

22. Shu(r) gu kong jong wu su(r)

23. Wu SHOW si-UNG sing shu(r)

24. Wu YUN-ar bee shu(r) SHEN yee

25. Wu su(r) sheng si-UNG way CHOO fah

26. Wu yun je-EH

27. NAY juh wu yee shu(r) je-EH

28. Wu wu ming

29. Yee wu wu MING jin

30. Nay juh wu LAO su(r)

31. Yee wu LAO su(r) JIN

32. WU ku juh me-EH dow

33. WU juh yee WU de(r)

34. Yee wu su-oh de(r) gu

35. POO tee SAH dwoh yee

36. BUN joh bwaw law ME dwaw

37. Gu SIN wu gu-ah AY

38. Wu gu-ah AY, gu wu YOH kong bu

39. Yu-en lee de-EN dao mung si-ung

40. Je-OO jing nee-EH pun

41. SUN shuh JU fah yee

42. Bun joh baw law ME du-aw

43. Gu de(r) AH no

44. Dwaw law SUN miao SUN poo tee.

45. Gu juh BUN joh bwaw law ME dwaw

46. Shu(r) DAH shen joh, shu(r) DAH ming joh

47. Shu(r) WU shung joh, shu(r) WU dung-dung joh

48. NUNG choo, yee chi-EH ku

49. JUN shu(r) BU su(r)

50. GU shu-oh BUN joh bwaw law ME dwaw joh

51. Juh shu-oh jo yu-EH

52. Je-EH dee, je-EH dee, bwaw law je-EH dee

53. Bwaw law sung je-EH dee

54. POO tee sah paw he(r)

GUT-tay GUT-tay PAHrah GUT-tay pah-rahSUM GUT-tay BO-dee SHVAH-ha

*Capitalized syllables are stressed.

**The (r) shown in parentheses is not strongly pronounced, but used as a guide to pronounce the preceding vowel as if the letter were there. Thus he(r) and shu(r) are pronounced somewhat as "her" and "shur" with almost no emphasis on the "r" sound.

CHAPTER 20 ~ The Practice of Kuan Yin's Rituals & Mantras
by Christine Meiner

Monks and sages have said that when using traditional mantras to Kuan Yin, we draw upon the energy momentum of millions of recitations uttered through the centuries, harnessing the tremendous power that these mantras now carry. (This ties in with modern morphic-field theories.) With such a great release of creative light, it is important to establish inner harmony before starting these rituals.

Kuan Yin's Ten Vows

These vows were taken from the Dharani Sutra, in which the Bodhisattva of Compassion invites all to make these vows with her and to her. Establishing a heart tie to Kuan Yin through these vows allows her to support us with more light. The Chinese word for vow, "yuan," also means "to wish" and "to want." Our thoughts, what our minds dwell on, become our vows, in that they direct our creative powers, our words and our feelings.

The Thirty-Three Manifestations of Kuan Yin

These powerful Chinese mantras are derived from ancient sacred texts. Originally written in Sanskrit, the *Lotus Sutra*, the *Shurangama Sutra* and the *Karandavyuha Sutra* describe various forms or manifestations of a divine being. These manifestations were introduced into the Chinese tradition through art, scripture and legend. Today they most closely correspond to thirty-three iconographic forms of Avalokitesvara (Kuan Yin) in Sino-Japanese art from the Kamakura period (1185–1333).

Kuan Yin offers these thirty-three manifestations of herself as antidotes to any challenges we may face in life. These mantras are presented in the next chapter (Part II of the ritual) along with the descriptive interpretations. Each image represents a form she has been known to assume in order to perform "tasks of salvation." Though her actual forms are numberless, each of these thirty-three manifestations carries the key to the resolution of a particular challenge or difficulty. Scholars still argue about the correct interpretations of some of these forms, so the true meaning of these manifestations for us individually is probably best gleaned from personal communication with our higher self. They also represent the thirty-three levels of testing we are required to pass to overcome and transcend our lower self.

In addition to the thirty-three manifestations, the 25th chapter of the Lotus Sutra, known as the Kuan Yin Sutra, states that Kuan Yin has the power to bestow protection from thirteen types of impending dangers upon devotees who meditate upon her essence, use the mantras frequently and maintain a practice of compassion. The *Surangama Sutra* promises that Kuan Yin can confer fourteen kinds of fearlessness upon devotees reciting these mantras. Fearlessness may break the law of karma because faith opens the door to possibilities previously not available to us.

In the ritual that follows in Chapter 21, the words to be recited are the phonetic pronunciations of the Chinese provided in bold-italic under each of the Chinese transliterations. You may sometimes choose to recite the English translations. Understanding the meanings can help us to powerfully visualize and direct the light for creative purposes.

You may also choose to use the Thirty-Three Manifestations of Kuan Yin as a *sadhana*, a contemplative rite involving visualization, in the following manner:

Visualize yourself in the center of the face of a large clock with twelve o'clock above you and six o'clock at your feet. Feel yourself drawing down the essence of Kuan Yin as a violet-pink light embodying her loving presence. For each repetition of the mantra, visualize violet, purple, pink, magenta and/or lavender light streaming forth from your heart to each hour-line on the clock, starting at 1 o'clock, proceeding clockwise so that the set of twelve repetitions ends at 12 o'clock.

Esoteric Buddhist legend states that twelve guardian devas protect the twelve directions and thirty-three beings guard the heavenly palace where the Buddha dwells. A celestial being at the center governs the other thirty-two beings who live in the Palace of Correct Views.

Place your attention on each line of the clock while moving your eyes clockwise. This action accesses various areas of the brain and various karmic memories. It results in a clearing action removing burdens from the soul.

Each line of the clock represents an aspect of misqualified energy, a certain way in which past misuses of energy could return and affect your world unless transmuted by the spiritual frequencies of the violet-light group or by loving service.

Strive toward maintaining stillness and experience the flow of forgiving love through your entire being. The purpose of reciting the words from a Dharani is to establish a divine interchange of energy between heavenly beings and the devotee.

It is important to begin your day and every spiritual practice by requesting and visualizing a sphere of dazzling light all around you to raise your energy vibration, strengthening your auric field.

This ritual may be used in its entirety or in part. Use your own attunement. The Great Compassion Mantra is traditionally done either once, 5 times, 21 times or 108 times daily. Mala beads have 108 beads and the big bead at the beginning is called the meru. When your fingers reach this bead after completing one circuit, the mala can be reversed and the movement continued in the opposite direction. With regular use, your rosary or mala beads become a repository for spiritual energy.

By consciously directing the flow of forgiving love as the Flame of Grace, in visualization and in our words, feelings and actions, we can create miracles. Bless life and be blessed by using this panacea which is a gift from the heart of our beloved Kuan Yin!

CHAPTER 21 ~ **The Thirty-Three Miracle Mantra Ritual**
by Christine Meiner

I ~ Kuan Yin's Ten Vows

Om Mani Beme Hum (5x)

[Ohm mahnee baymay hum]

Om...

Beloved Kuan Yin, how may I serve you today? Om...

1. In deepest reverence to the greatly compassionate Kuan Shih Yin, may I soon embody the teachings of the Buddha:

   Namo da bei Kuan Shih Yin, yuan wo su zhi yi qie fa! (5x)
   [NAH-moh dah bay Gwan Shu(r) EEN, yu-EN waw soo juh ee chi-eh FAH]*

   Om...

2. In deepest reverence to the greatly compassionate Kuan Shih Yin, may I swiftly attain the wisdom of inner vision:

   Namo da bei Kuan Shih Yin, yuan wo zao de zhi hui yan! (5x)
   [NAH-moh dah bay Gwan Shu(r) EEN, yu-EN waw zao duh juh hway yen]

   Om...

3. In deepest reverence to the greatly compassionate Kuan Shih Yin, may I quickly ferry all beings to the shore of liberation:

   Namo da bei Kuan Shih Yin, yuan wo su du yi qie jong! (5x)
   [NAH-moh dah bay Gwan Shu(r) EEN, yu-EN waw soo doo ee chi-EH jong]   Om...

163

4. In deepest reverence to the greatly compassionate Kuan Shih Yin, may I soon obtain good, expedient means to enlightenment:

Namo da bei Kuan Shih Yin, yuan wo zao de shan fang bian! (5x)
[NAH-moh dah bay Gwan Shu(r) EEN, yu-EN waw zao duh shahn fahng be-EN]

Om...

5. In deepest reverence to the greatly compassionate Kuan Shih Yin, may I swiftly board the boat of transcendental wisdom:

Namo da bei Kuan Shih Yin, yuan wo su cheng bo ru chuan! (5x)
[NAH-moh dah bay Gwan Shu(r) EEN, yu-EN waw SOO chung baw ROO chwun]

Om...

6. In deepest reverence to the greatly compassionate Kuan Shih Yin, may I soon transcend the sea of karmic suffering:

Namo da bei Kuan Shih Yin, yuan wo zao de yue ku hai! (5x)
[NAH-moh dah bay Gwan Shu(r) EEN, yu-EN waw zao duh yu-EH koo high]

Om...

7. In deepest reverence to the greatly compassionate Kuan Shih Yin, may I quickly internalize higher principles, the consciousness of formless awareness, and the way of the Buddha:

Namo da bei Kuan Shih Yin, yuan wo su de jie ding dao! (5x)
[NAH-moh dah bay Gwan Shu(r) EEN, yu-EN waw soo duh jyeh ding dow]

Om...

8. In deepest reverence to the greatly compassionate Kuan Shih Yin, may I soon climb the mountain of ultimate enlightenment:

   Namo da bei Kuan Shih Yin, yuan wo zao deng nie pan shan! (5x)
   [NAH-moh dah bay Gwan Shu(r) EEN, yu-EN waw zao dung nyeh PAHN shahn]

   Om...

9. In deepest reverence to the greatly compassionate Kuan Shih Yin, may I abide in a state of non-duality:

   Namo da bei Kuan Shih Yin, yuan wo su hui wu wei she! (5x)
   [NAH-moh dah bay Gwan Shu(r) EEN, yu-EN waw soo hway woo way shu(r)]

   Om...

10. In deepest reverence to the greatly compassionate Kuan Shih Yin, may I soon unite with the body of all essence:

    Namo da bei Kuan Shih Yin, yuan wo zao tong fa xing shen! (5x)
    [NAH-moh dah bay Gwan Shu(r) EEN, yu-EN waw zao tong fah SHING shun]

    Om...

Quietly give thanks to the merciful heart of Kuan Yin for always hearing our prayers.

* * * * *

II ~ Thirty-Three Manifestations of Kuan Yin

Om Mani Beme Hum (12x)

[Ohm mahnee baymay hum]
Om...

In humble adoration I kneel and touch my forehead to the ground before beloved Kuan Yin in all her manifestations.

Give prayers to Kuan Yin for intercession in personal and planetary matters. You may also use the recommended visualizations in the previous chapter.

1. Wo xiang yang liu Guan Yin kou tou (12x) Om...
   [Waw shi-UNG* YUNG lee-oh Gwan Yin kow tow**] Ohm...

   In humble adoration I kneel and touch my forehead to the ground before **Kuan Yin Who Holds a Willow Branch**. *This image represents Kuan Yin's ability to dispel illness with her healing powers. It teaches us of healing and compassion gained through inner flexibility and non-judgment.*

2. Wo xiang long tou Guan Yin kou tou (12x) Om...
   [Waw shi-UNG LONG toh Gwan Yin kow tow] Ohm...

   In humble adoration I kneel and touch my forehead to the ground before **Dragon-Head Kuan Yin**. *This image speaks of Kuan Yin's unlimited powers to free us from lack and unnecessary suffering. It also teaches us how abundance and good fortune can be gained through gratitude.*

3. Wo xiang chi jing Guan Yin kou tou (12x) Om...
   [Waw shi-UNG CHUH(R)*** jing Gwan Yin kow tow] Ohm...

   In humble adoration I kneel and touch my forehead to the ground before **Kuan Yin Who Holds the Sutras**. *This image represents the deeper insights of spiritual teachings. It teaches understanding of both the*

166

impermanence and the eternality of this world and the practical application of true spiritual wisdom.

4. Wo xiang yuan guang Guan Yin kou tou (12x) Om...
   [Waw shi-UNG yu-EN gwung Gwan Yin kow tow] Ohm...

   In humble adoration I kneel and touch my forehead to the ground before **Kuan Yin of Complete Light**. *This image speaks of Light dispelling all perceived darkness and misfortune. It teaches us to increase the Light in our chakras and how intense fire can purge our lives and consciousness.*

5. Wo xiang you xi Guan Yin kou tou (12x) Om...
   [Waw shi-UNG yo SHEE Gwan Yin kow tow] Ohm...

   In humble adoration I kneel and touch my forehead to the ground before **Kuan Yin of Enjoyment**. *This image of the playful, lighthearted Kuan Yin speaks of her assistance to those on the path of enlightenment. It teaches us to be compassionate towards both our shortcomings and our victories.*

6. Wo xiang bai yi Guan Yin kou tou (12x) Om...
   [Waw shi-UNG BUY-yee Gwan Yin kow tow] Ohm...

   In humble adoration I kneel and touch my forehead to the ground before **White-Robed Kuan Yin**. *This image represents the virtuous Kuan Yin, a perfect embodiment of purity. It teaches us fearlessness and helps us to see each other as Kuan Yin sees us.*

7. Wo xiang lian wo Guan Yin kou tou (12x) Om...
   [Waw shi-UNG lee-en WAW Gwan Yin kow tow] Ohm...

   In humble adoration I kneel and touch my forehead to the ground before **Kuan Yin Who Sits on a Lotus Leaf**. *This image shows Kuan Yin as having complete dominion over any perceived darkness. It teaches us what is real and what is not and how to rise above all suffering.*

8. Wo xiang long jian Guan Yin kou tou (12x) Om...
   [Waw shi-UNG long jen Gwan Yin kow tow] Ohm...

In humble adoration I bow and touch my forehead to the ground before **Kuan Yin Who Views Waterfalls**. *This image protects us against fires and intense emotions. It teaches us to stay calm, not react to energies flung our way and to stay focused on the desired outcome.*

9. Wo xiang shi yao Guan Yin kou tou (12x) Om...
   [Waw shi-UNG SHUH(R) yao Gwan Yin kow tow] Ohm...

   In humble adoration I kneel and touch my forehead to the ground before **Kuan Yin Who Gives Medicine**. *This image helps to dispel disease and all other difficult circumstances. It teaches us about compassion and how to be free from anger.*

10. Wo xiang yu lan Guan Yin kou tou (12x) Om...
    [Waw shi-UNG YOO lahn Gwan Yin kow tow] Ohm...

    In humble adoration I kneel and touch my forehead to the ground before **Kuan Yin of the Fish Basket**. *This image speaks of saving lives and souls. It teaches us to be kind to all forms of life and when to sacrifice for the benefit of others.*

11. Wo xiang de wang Guan Yin kou tou (12x) Om...
    [Waw shi-UNG DUH wung Gwan Yin kow tow] Ohm...

    In humble adoration I kneel and touch my forehead to the ground before **Kuan Yin as King of Merit**. *This image is about accomplishments and a sense of spiritual worthiness. It teaches us of true virtues and how to become a person of integrity and spiritual refinement.*

12. Wo xiang shui yue Guan Yin kou tou (12x) Om...
    [Waw shi-UNG shway YUH(R) Gwan Yin kow tow] Ohm...

    In humble adoration I kneel and touch my forehead to the ground before **Kuan Yin of Moon and Water**. *This image speaks of cause and effect. It teaches us about reality, unreality and how our outer life is a reflection of some aspect of our own consciousness.*

13. Wo xiang yi ye Guan Yin kou tou (12x) Om...
[Waw shi-UNG YEE yeh Gwan Yin kow tow] Ohm...

In humble adoration I kneel and touch my forehead to the ground before **One- Leaf Kuan Yin.** *Floating upon a single leaf, Kuan Yin protects us from perishing in the astral sea. It teaches us to remain centered and how to master our subconscious energies.*

14. Wo xiang qing jing Guan Yin kou tou (12x) Om...
[Waw shi-UNG CHING jing Gwan Yin kow tow] Ohm...

In humble adoration I kneel and touch my forehead to the ground before **Blue-Throated Kuan Yin.** *This image protects us from various poisons. It teaches us to be mindful of our speech and to always be in a vibration of loving-kindness.*

15. Wo xiang wei de Guan Yin kou tou (12x) Om...
[Waw shi-UNG WAY duh Gwan Yin kow tow] Ohm...

In humble adoration I kneel and touch my forehead to the ground before **Kuan Yin of Power and Virtue.** *This image protects us from perceived oppressive authorities. It teaches us to focus our energies on expanding the good and pouring creative light into our goals.*

16. Wo xiang yan ming Guan Yin kou tou (12x) Om...
[Waw shi-UNG yen MING Gwan Yin kow tow] Ohm...

In humble adoration I kneel and touch my forehead to the ground before **Kuan Yin Who Extends Life.** *This image protects us from the fear of curses and poisons. It teaches us that Light is our protection and that by the Law of Attraction, harm always returns to its source.*

17. Wo xiang zhong bao Guan Yin kou tou (12x) Om...
[Waw shi-UNG JONG bao Gwan Yin kow tow] Ohm...

In humble adoration I kneel and touch my forehead to the ground before **Kuan Yin of Various Treasures.** *This image offers spiritual seekers inner fortification and protection from being overcome by various opposing* *forces. It teaches us to seek help when we have gone off course and that one person's prayer can make a difference for the many.*

18. Wo xiang yan hu Guan Yin kou tou (12x) Om...
    [Waw shi-UNG yen HOO Gwan Yin kow tow] Ohm...

    In humble adoration I kneel and touch my forehead to the ground before **Kuan Yin of the Rock Cave.** *This image offers protection from negative vibrations and negative perceptions. It teaches us how to properly care for our bodies and to guard the gate of consciousness.*

19. Wo xiang neng jing Guan Yin kou tou (12x) Om...
    [Waw shi-UNG nung JING Gwan Yin kow tow] Ohm...

    In humble adoration I kneel and touch my forehead to the ground before **Kuan Yin Who Calms.** *This image helps us to be centered. It teaches us how to overcome anger and ignorance and not to be moved by any appearance or experience.*

20. Wo xiang Anu Guan Yin kou tou (12x) Om...
    [Waw shi-UNG AH-noo Gwan Yin kow tow] Ohm...

    In humble adoration I kneel and touch my forehead to the ground before **Anu Kuan Yin.** *This image represents the sacred mountain lake Anu. The rivers flowing from the lake pour out heavenly blessings in every direction. It teaches us about the path of the Bodhisattva and bids us to spread the message of Kuan Yin's transmuting powers of mercy and forgiveness to the world.*

21. Wo xiang a mo ti Guan Yin kou tou (12x) Om...
    [Waw shi-UNG AH-mo tee Gwan Yin kow tow] Ohm...

    In humble adoration I kneel and touch my forehead to the ground before **Kuan Yin of Fearlessness.** *This image bestows fearlessness when in challenging circumstances. It teaches us to be filled with love and to guard against judging reality by what is perceived through the five senses.*

22. Wo xiang ye yi Guan Yin kou tou (12x) Om...
    [Waw shi-UNG YEH yee Gwan Yin kow tow] Ohm...

    In humble adoration I kneel and touch my forehead to the ground before **Leaf- Robed Kuan Yin.** *This image protects against disease and ensures longevity. It teaches us how to work with the forces of nature and how to gain wisdom through observing the manifestations of cosmic law.*

23. Wo xiang liu li Guan Yin kou tou (12x) Om...
    [Waw shi-UNG Lee-OH lee Gwan Yin kow tow] Ohm...

    In humble adoration I kneel and touch my forehead to the ground before **Vaidurya Kuan Yin.** *This image is for healing. It teaches us to use lapis lazuli for healing and to bless and pray for all suffering life.*

24. Wo xiang Duo Luo Guan Yin kou tou (12x) Om...
    [Waw shi-UNG DAW Law Gwan Yin kow tow] Ohm...

    In humble adoration I kneel and touch my forehead to the ground before **Tara Kuan Yin.** *This image is of the Mother of Salvation. It teaches us about the feminine aspect of God and to always view others with healing compassion.*

25. Wo xiang ge li Guan Yin kou tou (12x) Om...
    [Waw shi-UNG guh LEE Gwan Yin kow tow] Ohm...

    In humble adoration I kneel and touch my forehead to the ground before **Kuan Yin of the Clam.** *This image protects us from perceived harm. It teaches us how to overcome negative states of consciousness and how to open closed, unmoving hearts and situations.*

26. Wo xiang liu shi Guan Yin kou tou (12x) Om...
    [Waw shi-UNG lee-OH shuh(r) Gwan Yin kow tow] Ohm...

    In humble adoration I kneel and touch my forehead to the ground before **Kuan Yin of Six Hours.** *This image reminds us of Kuan Yin's omnipresence and omniscience. It teaches us mastery over time and about being present in the now.*

27. Wo xiang pu bei Guan Yin kou tou (12x) Om...
    [Waw shi-UNG poo BAY Gwan Yin kow tow] Ohm...

    In humble adoration I kneel and touch my forehead to the ground before **Kuan Yin of Universal Compassion.** *This image brings promises of an end to all suffering. It teaches us about compassion as the nexus between heaven and earth and how to attain enlightenment by actively practicing compassion.*

28. Wo xiang Ma Lang fu Guan Yin kou tou (12x) Om...
    [Waw shi-UNG Mah Lung FOO Gwan Yin kow tow] Ohm...

    In humble adoration I kneel and touch my forehead to the ground before **Kuan Yin Called the Wife of Ma-Lang.** *This image bids us to demonstrate the path to higher consciousness. It teaches discernment of spirits and prepares us to share our insights with others.*

29. Wo xiang he zhang Guan Yin kou tou (12x) Om...
    [Waw shi-UNG HUH(R) jung Gwan Yin kow tow] Ohm...

    In humble adoration I kneel and touch my forehead to the ground before **Kuan Yin of Prayer.** *This image represents dedication of one's life to a spiritual path. It teaches us about devotion and the Gifts of the Holy Spirit.*

30. Wo xiang yi ru Guan Yin kou tou (12x) Om...
    [Waw shi-UNG YEE roo Gwan Yin kow tow] Ohm...

    In humble adoration I kneel and touch my forehead to the ground before **Kuan Yin of Oneness.** *This image represents harmony. It teaches us to rise above the vibrations of this world and to remain centered when experiencing the appearance of negative energy.*

31. Wo xiang bu er Guan Yin kou tou (12x) Om...
    [Waw shi-UNG Boo-AHR Gwan Yin kow tow] Ohm...

    In humble adoration I kneel and touch my forehead to the ground before **Kuan Yin of Non-Duality.** *This image promises protection from* *perceived negative energies. It teaches us how to suspend judgment and conquer our belief in any internal or external division.*

32. Wo xiang chi lian hua Guan Yin kou tou (12x) Om...
    [Waw shi-UNG chuh(r) lee-en HWA Gwan Yin kow tow] Ohm...

    In humble adoration I kneel and touch my forehead to the ground before **Kuan Yin Holding a Lotus.** *This image represents the Vow of the Bodhisattva. It teaches us how to correctly perceive the need of the hour and to consciously work with the energies of our chakras.*

33. Wo xiang sa shui Guan Yin kou tou (12x) Om...
    [Waw shi-UNG SAH shway Gwan Yin kow tow] Ohm...

    In humble adoration I kneel and touch my forehead to the ground before **Kuan Yin Who Sprinkles Pure Water.** *This image represents the many blessings of Kuan Yin. It teaches us about the healing, transforming powers of forgiveness, mercy and compassion.*

Quietly give thanks to the merciful heart of Kuan Yin for always hearing our prayers.

Remember, these mantras can also be done individually when a specific action is needed.

*Capitalized syllables are stressed.

**Both "kow" and "tow" rhyme with the word "cow."

***The (r) shown in parentheses is not strongly pronounced, but used as a guide to pronounce the preceding vowel as if the letter were there. Thus he(r) and shu(r) are pronounced somewhat as "her" and "shur" with almost no emphasis on the "r" sound.

CHAPTER 22 ~ **More Mantras & Prayers for Personal & Global Transformation**

1. Om Amitabha hri
   [Ohm AH-mee-TAH-bah* hree]
   Mantra to the Dhyani Buddha Amitabha.

2. Namo Kuan Zhi Zai P'u Sa
   [NAH-moh Gwun Juh ZY Poo Sah]
   I honor Kuan Yin who observes the Ultimate Nature of Reality.

3. Namo bai yi da shih
   [NAH-moh buy ee dah shuh(r)**]
   I honor the white-robed, honored one.

4. Namo Kuan Shih Yin P'u Sa
   [NAH-moh Gwun Shuh(r) EEN Poo Sah]
   I honor Kuan Yin, Bodhisattva.

5. Namo da bei Kuan Shih Yin P'u Sa
   [NAH-moh dah bay Gwun Shuh(r) EEN Poo Sah]
   I honor the greatly pitying Bodhisattva Kuan Shih Yin.

6. Chiu ku chiu nan P'u Sa lai
   [Je-OH koo je-OH nun Poo Sah ly]
   Save from suffering, save from disaster. Bodhisattva, come!

7. Namo tzu bei ta shih
   [NAH-moh tsuh bay DAH shuh(r)]
   I honor the compassionate and pitying honored one.

8. Namo a-li-yeh, To-Lo
   [NAH-moh AH-lee-yeh Daw-Law]
   I honor the sagely one, Tara.

9. Namo chien shou chien yen Kuan Shih Yin P'u Sa
   [NAH-moh chee-EN shoh chee-EN yen Gwun Shuh(r) EEN Poo Sah]
   I honor the thousand-armed, thousand-eyed Bodhisattva Kuan Shih Yin.

10. Om tare tuttare ture svaha!
    [Ohm TAH-ray TOO-tah-ray TOO-ray svah-HAH]
    One interpretation of Tara's mantra: Hail to you, Tara, the embodiment of all the Buddhas' actions. I honor you always with my body, speech and mind, whether I am in happy or unhappy circumstances.

11. Namo liu li Kuan Yin
    [NAH-moh lee-OH lee Gwun EEN]
    I honor the Vaidurya Lapis Lazuli Kuan Yin.
    Give this mantra a thousand times a day (it takes about 20 minutes) for thirty-three or forty days. It is called the Miracle Mantra.

12. Namo yang liu Kuan Yin
    [NAH-moh yung lee-OH Gwun EEN]
    I honor **Kuan Yin Who Holds the Willow Branch**.
    Use this for healing.

13. Namo i ju Kuan Yin
    [NAH-moh ee roo Gwun EEN]
    I honor **Kuan Yin of Oneness**.
    Antidote to war, hurricanes, weather, etc.

14. Om Tam Tara-aye Namaha
    [Ohm TUM TAH-rah-AY NUM-ah-ha]
    Om! Power in the great name of Tara!

   *Capitalized syllables are stressed.

   **The (r) shown in parentheses is not strongly pronounced, but used as a guide to pronounce the preceding vowel as if the letter were there. Thus he(r) and shu(r) are pronounced somewhat as "her" and "shur" with almost no emphasis on the "r" sound.

Kuan Yin Hand Mantras

Adapted from the 42 Hands (Mudras) in the Dharani Sutra

1. Wo xiang ju i chu shou Guan Yin kou tou
   [Waw shi-UNG* ROO ee DJOO shoh GWUN Yin kow tow**]

   I reverently touch my forehead to the ground before **Kuan Yin of the As-You-Will-Pearl Hand.**
   Use for prosperity, abundance, to find gems, etc.

2. Wo xiang bao bo shou Guan Yin kou tou
   [Waw shi-UNG BAO baw shoh GWUN Yin kow tow]

   I reverently touch my forehead to the ground before **Kuan Yin of the Jeweled-Bowl Hand.**
   Use for healing illness. Charge water with this mantra or with The Great Compassion Mantra.

3. Wo xiang jih ching mo ni shou Guan Yin kou tou
   [Waw shi-UNG JUH jing MWOH nee shoh GWUN Yin kow tow]

   I reverently touch my forehead to the ground before **Kuan Yin of the Sun-Essence Mani [Jewel] Hand.**
   Use for healing the eyes.

4. Wo xiang bao chien shou Guan Yin kou tou
   [Waw shi-UNG BAO je-EN shoh GWUN Yin kow tow]

   I reverently touch my forehead to the ground before ***Kuan Yin of the Jeweled-Arrow Hand***.
   Use for making good friends.

5. Wo xiang bai fu shou Guan Yin kou tou
   [Waw shi-UNG BUY foo shoh GWUN Yin kow tow]

176

I reverently touch my forehead to the ground before **Kuan Yin of the White-Whisk Hand**.
Use for dissipating obstacles.

6. Wo xiang yueh fu shou Guan Yin kou tou
   [Waw shi-UNG yoo-EH foo shoh GWUN Yin kow tow]

   I reverently touch my forehead to the ground before **Kuan Yin of the Ax Hand.**
   Use for avoiding problems with the law and imprisonment.
   Use for help in all legal affairs.

7. Wo xiang bai lien shou Guan Yin kou tou
   [Waw shi-UNG BUY lee-EN shoh GWUN Yin kow tow]

   I reverently touch my forehead to the ground before **Kuan Yin of the White-Lotus Hand**.
   Use for increasing virtue.

8. Wo xiang bao chieh shou Guan Yin kou tou
   [Waw shi-UNG BAO chee-EH shoh GWUN Yin kow tow]

   I reverently touch my forehead to the ground before **Kuan Yin of the Jewel-Chest Hand**.
   Use for finding treasures in the earth.

9. Wo xiang wu se yun shou Guan Yin kou tou
   [Waw shi-UNG WU suh yoon shoh GWUN Yin kow tow]

   I reverently touch my forehead to the ground before **Kuan Yin of the Five-Colored-Cloud Hand.**
   Use for alleviating sorrow.

10. Wo xiang bao chi shou Guan Yin kou tou
    [Waw shi-UNG BAO jee shoh GWUN Yin kow tow]

    I reverently touch my forehead to the ground before **Kuan Yin of the Jeweled-Halberd Hand**.
    Use for protection of your country from invading enemies.

11. Wo xiang ho chang shou Guan Yin kou tou
    [Waw shi-UNG HUH jung shoh GWUN Yin kow tow]

    I reverently touch my forehead to the ground before **Kuan Yin of the Joined-Palms Hand**.
    Use for people to treat each other with love and respect.

12. Wo xiang bao ching shou Guan Yin kou tou
    [Waw shi-UNG BAO jing shoh GWUN Yin kow tow]

    I reverently touch my forehead to the ground before **Kuan Yin of the Jeweled-Sutra Hand.**
    Use for learning, study, memory and wisdom.

*Capitalized syllables are stressed.

**Both "kow" and "tow" rhyme with the word "cow."

Mudras—Gestures of Power

The understanding of the power of mudra dates back to ancient Egypt from where it spread eastward. This knowledge has generally disappeared along with much of the esoteric sciences of the past, but some of it does survive in parts of India and Tibet.

Different types of awareness can be accessed through symbolic pass codes. The symbols can be images, gestures, and teraphim or talismans. They can be a transcendental link to inner spiritual worlds and also to higher feeling states. The sages recognized that mudras can access and actualize many qualities like compassion, fearlessness, joy, enlightenment and almost any quality we aspire to when performed. The mind, body and feelings are interconnected. A good example of this is that even smiling generates measurable positive changes in the heart and bodily functions.

Some older versions of the Dharani purportedly have the powerful mudras (sacred gestures) associated with these mantras that are listed in Chapter 14. Ask Kuan Yin to perform the mudras for you as you recite the mantras. It's best to do them in multiples of 33, 40 or 108, and always remember to ask that your prayer requests be adjusted to be in accordance with the will of God.

Bhumisparsha (Earth Touching) Mudra. This mudra evokes Gautama Buddha's enlightenment under the bodhi tree, when he summoned the Earth Goddess, Sthavara, to bear witness to his attainment of enlightenment. The right hand, placed near the right knee with fingers touching the earth, is complemented by the left hand held flat in the lap in the dhyana mudra of meditation. These symbolize the union of samasara (this world of illusion) with nirvana. It is in this posture that Shakyamuni overcame the obstructions of Mara while meditating on Truth. The second Dhyani Buddha Akshobhya is depicted in this mudra. He is believed to transform the delusion of anger into mirror-like wisdom.

~ ADDITIONAL INVOCATIONS ~

Daily Call for Protection

O my beloved individualized Divine Presence, the great I Am That I Am, place an impenetrable sphere of white light all around me now. Blaze your violet fire within it to consume my negative records. I ask Archangel Michael to place a blue sphere around the outer periphery for additional protection from negative forces!

Short Prayer to Kuan Yin

Beloved Kuan Yin, I call for your compassion to ignite and amplify in every human heart on this earth!

Prayer for Planetary Mercy

Beloved Kuan Yin and all the Legions of Light serving this planet, saturate the earth and all life on it with oceans of mercy. Transmute all hardness of heart and evil intent, consume all negative energies and records, and cut free both mankind and animal life from all forms of abuse and cruelty. Cleanse the earth and all thereon. Protect and rescue all those serving the Light. Let love and freedom prevail on this planet and let this prayer be sustained and amplified forever.

I Am the Light of the Heart
from The Summit Lighthouse

I Am the Light of the Heart
Shining in the darkness of being
And changing all into the golden treasury
Of the Mind of Christ.
I Am projecting my Love
Out into the world
To erase all errors

181

And to break down all barriers.
I Am the power of infinite Love,
Amplifying Itself
Until It is victorious,
World without end!

Violet Fire Decree
from The Summit Lighthouse

I Am forgiveness acting here
Lasting out all doubt and fear
Setting men forever free
With wings of cosmic victory.
I Am calling in full power
For forgiveness every hour
To all life in every place
I flood forth forgiving grace

Violet Fire Mantra
from The Summit Lighthouse

I Am a being of violet fire
I Am the purity God desires!

This short mantra can be easily memorized and done throughout the day. It is also recommended to be done often in many variations, such as:

Earth is a planet of violet fire
Earth is the purity God desires!

America is a land of violet fire
America is the purity God desires!

You can substitute any nation, city, school, person, pet, situation, etc. in this mantra. Be creative and use it daily. The word purple can also be used instead of violet at any time. Purple is said to have a more cleansing frequency, while violet is considered to be more aligned with mercy.

Decrees and mantras are usually done in multiples of three to access the power of the Three-Times-Three multiplication. At the end of any mantra or prayer session, request that it all be multiplied by the power of the 3x3, 10x10, 10,000x10,000, the power of the square (multiplied by itself) and every dispensation of multiplication allowed at this time.

My teachers have said that prayers and mantras are also multiplied by the square of the number of people doing them in unison. For example, if you have a group of three, the multiplication factor is 9; if there are 10 people, it would be 100. That's why it is so beneficial to organize a regular family or group session.

CHAPTER 23 ~ **The Multiplication Power of the Prayer Wheel**

Prayer wheels come in many sizes and have been used for centuries.

The prayer wheel was introduced into Tibet from India by Padmasambhava in the 8th century. The monk Nagajuna started the practice in India in the first century BCE at the behest of Avalokitesvara but its origins are considered to be much older. It was given by Avalokitesvara for the swift clearing of past offenses and for the ultimate liberation of all sentient beings. It proliferated through many Asian countries in the 18th and 19th centuries, but has only been spreading in the West since the 1990s. It is not a wheel, but a cylinder containing mantras on paper or microfilm. Because the mantra is frequently *Om Mani Padme Hum*, it is also called the mani wheel or lotus wheel.

There are several types of these cylinders, such as the fire wheel, wind wheel, water wheel, ground wheel and hand wheel, depending on how and where they are powered and turned. Some are huge, requiring several people to turn, while others are small, hand-held or desktop devices. The multiplication factor is figured by the number of mantras inside and by the number of rotations of the wheel. Many now contain microfilm as this greatly increases the number inside. Each time the wheel is turned, the supplicant accumulates the benefit of chanting the number of mantras that are written inside the cylinder. If it contains 100,000 mantras, as some do, ten turns equals one million recitations!

Prayer wheels need to be both constructed and filled correctly according to specifications. Many available through catalogs and stores are not correct, with mantras even upside down or backwards, which, of course, will not produce the desired effect. Hand-held ones also need to be turned correctly, held upright and twirled clockwise in a steady motion while reciting the mantra. The left hand usually counts on mala beads, and the right hand turns the wheel. It should never be held obliquely, sideways or upside down.

The Benefits

Prayer wheel usage was endorsed by the great ones like Maitreya, Manjushri, Padmasambhava and Milarepa among others. The following is only a partial list of the numerous traditional benefits attributed:

- It purifies the mind and body

- Turning the prayer wheel even once with correct motivation and recitation accumulates more merit than years of spiritual retreat

- Eliminates negative tendencies and amplifies good qualities

- Accelerates transmutation of negative karma

- Protects from disease

- Counteracts opposition from dark forces

- Creates peaceful surroundings around the wheel

- Helps develop compassion, joy and kindness

- Promotes mastery of relationships, prosperity and sustenance

- Eliminates obstacles

- Enables more effective meditation

- Facilitates rebirth in higher realms

- Seeing, touching or hearing a prayer wheel can bestow benefits such as future enlightenment

- Having one in your home makes it an equivalent to the pure land of Kuan Yin

Techniques & Visualizations

Begin with reverence to Kuan Yin and recite:

Namo Kuan Yin, Bodhisattva of Compassion,

Om Mani Padme Hum

I desire to free all beings and all creatures from suffering and ignorance!

Next, while turning the wheel clockwise, recite the *Om Mani Padme Hum*, preferably 1,000 times or more, counting ten rounds on your mala beads. (Ten times 108 on the beads is 1,080 times, which takes about twenty minutes.) Visualize the light beams that are emitted from the wheel dissolving your karma and all the negative energy records from yourself and the planet. See the light piercing all dimensions, even the underworld, and erasing all darkness and suffering. Then see the inhabitants of the various realms developing love and joy.

Visualize the light rays comforting all animals and creatures, freeing them from suffering. See all darkness and evil absorbed into the prayer wheel, then dissolved and transmuted into light.

If you wish, when you are done, you may dedicate all virtue from your practice to the saving of the earth and the liberation of all beings from suffering and ignorance. This is a customary dedication in many parts of the Orient.

Specifications for correct construction of prayer wheels can be found in Lorne Ladner's *Wheel of Great Compassion*. It also contains mantras to photocopy and wrap around the central shaft. Prayer wheels can also be found in stores and online, but try to confirm the source of manufacture to get the genuine article.

CHAPTER 24 ~ **Powerful Meditations**

Why meditate? Studies show that meditation yields many physical, mental and emotional health benefits, as well as improves behavior and relationships. It also helps relieve stress and lightens dark moods, reduces pain and has a positive impact on blood pressure and the body's chemical and hormonal balance.

The benefits are cumulative. It can lead to serenity, mental clarity, insight and the experience of samadhi, which is a profound stillness of mind. Meditation brings self-knowledge and opens the mind and heart, thereby dissolving the barriers that keep us from connecting with others at a deep heart level. It can be spiritually transformative and can result in the highest bliss, enlightenment and connection with spiritual beings.

Meditation is a mental and spiritual discipline of concentration and focused awareness through which we access different states and levels of consciousness, uniting heart and mind. It is not thinking, nor is it an intellectual exercise. It goes beyond mental concepts to direct experience and direct knowing in a form that is inaccessible to the thinking mind. When we meditate, we become aware of our union with the Divine.

There are many methods and techniques and each person has to find out what he or she is best suited for through trial and error. The eighth level of samadhi is the point of directly experiencing the universe as pure consciousness and everything in it as a manifestation of the Infinite One. According to some traditions, liberation is attained at the ninth level. Each successive level becomes more difficult to conceptualize and impossible to verbalize.

In Mark Prophet's *Prayer and Meditation*, Master Kuthumi says, "In prayer, man makes intercession to God for assistance; in meditation, he gives assistance to God by creating the nature of God within his own thoughts and feelings. Meditate, then, with the idea of plunging into the ocean of God."

Meditation Posture

Meditation can be done walking, sitting, standing or lying down. The traditional crosslegged, seated position was not an arbitrary choice but is used because it is the most effective in achieving the purposes of meditation, as body position affects consciousness. Generally speaking, meditation can be a lot more difficult without this posture, which is naturally conducive to the meditative process.

Although we strive to maintain stillness in this position, stiffness and rigidity are to be avoided because they increase tension and cause pain. It is more of a flexible stillness without fidgeting, like a tree that moves almost imperceptibly in the wind.

The spine should be aligned like a stack of blocks which cannot collapse because it is directly in line with the force of gravity. If the vertebrae are not aligned vertically with gravity, it requires muscle tension to keep the spine from slumping. Tension in the body leads to tension in the mind and both will interfere with meditation, so the idea is to become as relaxed as possible in the vertical position. This is an ongoing process, not a one-time achievement. Eventually correct posture requires only a small amount of effort to maintain.

A major key to achieving this almost effortless verticality lies in keeping the knees lower than the hips. If you look at pictures of people seated in meditation, you'll notice their knees are never up in the air. No matter which cross-legged position is used, the knees are down so the pelvis can tilt forward a little and the weight of the torso can be maintained above the "sit bones." This is the reason for the various meditation seats and cushions available on the market.

Achieving good balance in this position can be a meditation in itself; it's a process of continual refinement. The mind becomes stilled, no longer preoccupied with incessant commentary, and the heart is open, paving the way for joy and compassion.

Sages of the past found that the practice and mastery of this posture naturally leads to altered states of higher consciousness. Meditation is a cross-cultural, non-denominational practice that can be used by anyone to progress on their chosen spiritual path.

That being said about traditional posture, I have to admit that my highest meditation experiences have occurred when out in nature on sunny days, walking in the woods or along a stream. I begin with emptying the mind of all words and commentary, maintaining wordless observation both within and without, then shift to meditating on oneness or connection with my higher Self. The direct experience arrives for me with a burst of light and bliss.

The Meditations

Before doing the following or any meditation, remember to first visualize a sphere or cylinder of white light around you and ask Archangel Michael for his protection. It's important to shield yourself from any entities or dark forces that might be attracted to or oppose your light.

Kuan Yin's Sound Meditation

In the *Shurangama Sutra*, Kuan Yin revealed this meditation as the one that led to her ultimate enlightenment, liberation, vast powers, and ability to manifest in 32 additional forms.

Select a spot either indoors or outdoors where you will be uninterrupted for a while. Seat yourself comfortably in a chair or in the cross-legged meditation posture. Relax and empty your mind by focusing your attention on your breath or into your limbs or torso. Ignore any thoughts that arise. Now turn your attention to the sounds in your environment. Just listen with pure awareness without attaching words or meaning to what you hear. Listen to the silence between sounds. By and by, you discover that both sound and silence are objects of the sense of hearing, but are not real hearing. You become aware of being separate from both sound and hearing and move on to listening to yourself hearing. Eventually you move beyond the duality of sound and silence, beyond hearing into conscious awareness where sound has disappeared and you become aware of the Source of hearing, which is not the body.

Kuan Yin said that bit-by-bit, both hearing and what is heard will vanish. Then even the awareness of silence vanishes. Then both awareness of this state and the state itself are realized as empty, as having no intrinsic, independent existence. Consciousness merges with the all-embracing Void, and all duality disappears. She says that by this method, "I suddenly transcended both the physical and spiritual realms and there was brightness in every direction."

Kuan Yin's meditation is traditionally considered the best route for the average person to transcend the mundane world if they persevere with regular practice and allow the process to unfold naturally.

Violet Light Meditation

Both thought and color have wavelengths that affect your physical body and its etheric envelope. Your etheric body is an energy field that can be seen by clairvoyants and photographed by Kirlian photography. Dr. John Ott who did research in color with time-lapse photography showed that different colors have different physical effects on people and plants.

Get into your preferred meditation position and close your eyes. Focus on your breath for a few minutes to clear your mind of thought. When you're ready, visualize yourself in a sphere of violet light. Visualize yourself inhaling it through your nose and also simultaneously absorbing it through your skin. Your entire body is absorbing this light.

While holding your in-breath, mentally direct the violet light to whatever part of your body you want to help or heal. On a gentle out-breath, breathe out tension, energy blocks and unwanted conditions and see them dissolve in the violet light. Continue as long as it feels comfortable. You may use other colors from the violet group, or different hues of greens or other pastel colors. Once you feel you've accomplished this for yourself, you can expand it to include your family, neighborhood, town, state and country—eventually the entire planet.

Summer Lawnchair Samadhi Meditation

The first level of samadhi can be reached when relaxing alone while reclining in a lawnchair in your backyard or at a campsite. Samadhi is a non-dualistic state of consciousness where thinking has been replaced by pure awareness.

As usual, begin by emptying the mind of thought. Focus attention on your breathing, either in your heart, or at the point just below your nose, or at the third eye. Breath observation deepens relaxation and the meditation process. After a while, begin to observe your surroundings without commentary. Gently dismiss any thoughts by returning to wordless awareness and keep your consciousness further back than you normally do. If it's normally right behind your eyes, move it back more. Watch yourself watching the world. Merge with that consciousness that observes yourself observing. With practice, the sense of separation dissolves into a delightful sense of unity with everything. Avoid effort, allow it to happen naturally. The experience of oneness does not come from thought, but by the relinquishing of thought, which creates the right conditions.

Forgiveness Meditation

This can be done anytime, anywhere. Picture yourself in a cylinder of magenta light. Think of someone who is or has been a problem or an annoyance for you. See this person also surrounded by a tube of magenta light. Now visualize a cascading waterfall of dazzling pink and violet light pouring down over both of you. Visualize this light dissolving and consuming the issues within and between you both. Smile at each other. See your hearts smiling at each other. See that person as an expression of the Infinite One in embodiment. Feel compassion for the One in that embodiment. Realize you are both manifestations of the One. Ask Kuan Yin, your Higher Self, or the violet-light angels to dissolve and transmute all past negative energies and records between you and this person. When you feel ready, release this person into the light.

Now you may choose someone else and repeat the process. Continue as long as you wish. According to crystal teacher Robert Simmons, Celestite is an

192

invaluable meditation aid for reaching higher consciousness and accessing the energies of forgiveness.

Saint Germain's Meditation

Saint Germain recommended this as a daily meditation in *Unveiled Mysteries* through Godfre Ray King:

Assume your preferred meditation position. Relax physically with your awareness focused on the breath as it enters and exits your body just below the nose. Clear the mind of thought and commentary by maintaining wordless awareness of yourself and your surroundings.

When you are ready, visualize and feel yourself surrounded and infused by brilliant white light. While maintaining this image, picture a golden light in your heart and focus your awareness there. Establish a feeling of connection to the Divine Presence within.

After about five minutes, feel the Light increasing in every part of your body and enter into an expanded acceptance of and immersion into the Divine. Continue this for about ten more minutes. End your meditation with I Am affirmations of Light such as "I Am Light," "I Am cleansed by Light," "I Am a Sun," etc.

CHAPTER 25 ~ Ho'oponopono: The Hawaiian Forgiveness Method

with Boyd Badten's Forgiveness Meditation

I asked Boyd Badten, a friend from Livingston, Montana, with a strong spiritual attunement if he'd like to contribute his compassion meditation for this book. When Boyd goes into deep meditation on compassion, or any other quality, for thirty or more minutes, it becomes such a tangible force that he can move it out into the world with his hands. He felt guided to share his version of the Ho'oponopono meditation, so I'll first give some background on this for those who are not familiar with it.

Ho'oponopono (pronounced *ho-oh pono pono*) means "to cause to make right." It is an ancient Hawaiian kahuna (shamanic) system of forgiveness, transmutation and healing updated into a more practical system for modern times by Morrnah Nalamaku Simeona. Morrnah has performed many healing miracles through this technique.

This topic fits neatly into a book on Kuan Yin, because love and forgiveness are the heart of ho'oponopono and also the heart of the mercy and compassion that Kuan Yin expects us to extend to others (and ourselves) when we request her intercession and recite her mantras.

The first concept is that we take responsibility for anything negative that appears in our life and "make it right." This includes any problem that comes to our attention regardless of its source—from relatives, clients, books, the news media—whatever. If it's on our radar, it's up for transformation and we can do the job. It doesn't matter who has the problem, or how we found out about it, or whether the problem is personal or global. If it's in our sphere of awareness, it's our problem, too! Taking responsibility (the ability to respond) does not necessarily mean taking the blame, but it does mean doing something to transmute the shared energy in the collective consciousness.

This ties in to the second concept that the conditions coming to our attention or into our life are the outpicturing of something in our subconscious.

The third concept is that if it is transmuted within us, it is also no longer "out there" either, as it has been eradicated from the collective unconscious. Once a fault or a problem and its cause are no longer in us at some level, even as an ancient record, we no longer perceive it in another. I'm surmising that this is because we are all connected at a deep level, which ties in to the Mayan recognition of the fact that "you are another me."

As scientists now postulate that we live in a holographic universe where the whole is contained in every part, and the part is everywhere in the whole, then you, too, are part of the whole. So when you neutralize an energy record in you, it is neutralized everywhere in the whole. Since everything in the universe is composed of energy and wave information, this can occur easily.

I don't know Morrnah's full technique, but she used the following prayer and taught it to others as an important step in her forgiveness and healing method:

"Divine Creator—Father, Mother and Son as One—if I, my family, relatives and ancestors have offended you, your family, relatives, and ancestors, in thoughts, words, deeds and actions from the beginning of our creation to the present, we ask your forgiveness. Let this cleanse, purify, release, cut all the negative memories, blocks, energies and vibrations and transmute these unwanted energies into pure light. And it is done."

Dr. Ihaleakala Hew Len who teaches Ho'oponopono workshops shares this prayer with people:

I love you,
I'm sorry,
Please forgive me,
Thank you.

We can recite these phrases in any order, vary the wording as we wish, and repeat each line as often as we like. For example:

I love you so much,
I really love you,
Forgive me, please,

195

I am really very sorry,
I forgot you are an expression of the One.
And I'm very grateful, thank you.
Thank you so much!

Whatever feels right will work just fine. We can have long pauses between phrases or just repeat one or two phrases over and over. Some people like to just mentally repeat "I love you" all day long to everything and everyone or to the Divine. It's not just a matter of reciting the words, it's important to feel them. If we don't feel sincere at first, we can keep repeating them (either verbally or silently) in whatever form and order feels right, until it becomes sincere, then continue until we feel a shift and a release of the energies. Some situations may require continual daily repetition until the problem is resolved. Transmute the situation with heart-fire and Heartsound!

Note that we do this no matter who was seemingly the wrongdoer and even if we were the victims.

Most of the time, we are addressing the Divine. We can think of the Divine as the Higher Self directly above us, or we can address the Higher Self of another either above or within them. We're saying, "Please forgive whatever it is in me, at any level, that caused this to outpicture in the world. I'm so sorry and I really love you."

Even though we're not the murderer, drug dealer, liar, gossip monger, adulterer, or whatever the situation is, when we say these prayers, they work at the level of the collective consciousness. We're not directly trying to "fix" the other person or outer situation because, according to the Law of the One, whatever is cleansed in one is cleansed in the other, because there is only the One in manifestation, individuated as the many. This can be a difficult concept to grasp with the intellect, but it can be directly grasped in a meditation experience when we reach the point where duality disappears.

This method of prayer has been used successfully for many kinds of situations from finances, weight loss, health issues and relationships to global problems. For added momentum, try alternating the phrases with Kuan Yin mantras.

Boyd Badten's Ho'oponopono Forgiveness Meditation

I begin by relaxing my body and breathing very deeply and slowly, taking in and absorbing a much higher than normal amount of prana (life-force energy). After about 5 minutes, I focus my attention on my heart chakra and remember that the bright Light within my heart is the very Presence of God. With my inner vision I see this bright Light within my heart growing larger and brighter as my attention and devotion to the Presence of God within continues.

Soon I start to experience a swelling, burning, magnetic feeling in my heart chakra, and my consciousness begins to expand as the resonance increases between this higher part of myself/God and my outer waking consciousness. I continue to hold my attention upon my Higher Self until I feel myself expanded and melted into the One Undivided Life.

I gently hold myself here for some time in order to stabilize my waking brain consciousness in this extraordinarily expanded awareness while joyfully, rhythmically affirming that I Am one with the All in All.

I now turn my inner gaze back to the land of duality, where souls have their awareness entirely upon their dividedness, their separate individuality. I notice that this sense of division has caused souls to hurl dark energy and patterns of unkindness toward one another. Some have hurled their negativity with such vehemence that portions of their very souls have projected forth along with their missiles of unkindness. These soul parts, dark energy and jagged patterns have embedded themselves into their victims, causing distress, pain and sorrow. I see that this pain and sorrow is experienced by both the attacker and victim, yet each of them is, in reality, a drop in the ocean of the One Undivided Life.

A feeling of great compassion grows within me as I view these scenes multiplied millions of times over all the earth. I now actively choose to see all these souls as a part of the Ocean of Life which I AM. I actively feel the Light within each heart as one with the All-in-All. And as all things equal to the same thing are equal to each other, I feel all hearts dissolving into that Oneness which I continue to inhabit.

Holding this field of awareness of unity, I simultaneously begin to forgive and be forgiven, for I Am now both attacker and victim:

I Love You
I'm Sorry
Please Forgive Me
Thank You

I Love You—

I Am One with all life and I instantly feel the Love I Am expressing as both giver and receiver—Oh, what a joy!

I'm Sorry—

I forgot that we are One and I feel the pain that I gave to you/myself. Oh, feel my remorse and my desire to make everything shiny and happy again!

Please Forgive Me—

Oh, please let these dark arrows of pain be dissolved now! I release them/take them back to me and the love that I feel turns all back into Light!

Thank You—

I feel so grateful for this cosmic healing. I see now so clearly that all of life is one, and that all I ever send forth to another part of life is visited upon me, not by a wrathful God, but because there is only Me— the One Life:

I Love You
I'm Sorry
Please Forgive Me
Thank You

I Love You
I'm Sorry
Please Forgive Me
Thank You

Now my field of vision is filled with the lively action of millions of streams of energy, originally hurled in disparagement, relaxing their holds on unfortunate people, transforming into beautiful Light Forms and returning to the senders. Fragmented soul parts are warmed, shiny and clean in this tremendous Love Shower, and are returned to their rightful owners where the healing and integration continues by angels. Each one feels a new freedom and the opportunity to step forward—free from as much of the pain and burden they previously felt as is possible:

I Love You
I'm Sorry
Please Forgive Me
Thank You

Each repetition of this miracle meditation increases the action of freedom from past unkind thoughts, words and actions. If I focus upon a particular type of human interaction, for instance, the pain children feel when their parents fight and argue, I find that my attention is drawn to view millions of instances of this exact situation. I radiate my joy into these scenes:

I Love You
I'm Sorry
Please Forgive Me
Thank You

I see the energy patterns of pain and loneliness relax, unwind and become shiny and clean again! Now I see family members all over the earth who have not spoken for years. The litany of seeming injustices is visible in their auras and even their physical appearances. I affirm for, with and as them:

I Love You
I'm Sorry
Please Forgive Me
Thank You

Sometimes, a part of me wonders a little bit, can it be possible for me to cause all of this to happen? This is between other people. How can it be something that I can interfere in? But I reaffirm that I Am One with all of life and therefore, I can take responsibility for the pain and sorrow in the world. And if I am willing to take responsibility for it—to own it. I can indeed heal some part of it also:

I Love You...

~ *Afterword* ~
REMEMBER YOUR POWER TOOLS

In summary, here is a dynamic dozen of powerful tools to supercharge your spiritual growth, conscious awareness and joy:

1. The Power of ZERO POINT

Zero Point in the heart is both an interdimensional portal and a convergence point for all that is. Here we can connect with celestial beings and the Divine. Entering the heart with love and sacred sound toning—Heartsound—gives us the access code to Zero Point.

2. The Power of HEART INTELLIGENCE

When we let our consciousness enter the heart in a state of profound peace and serenity, we can seek guidance there. This is the place to ask for solutions, and the answers will come either quickly or in due time.

3. The Power of HEARTSOUND

Sound is a key creative force in the universe. Sound waves can be conducted in the brain, bones, organs and the chambers of the throat and head for healing. Toning mantras or vowels can stimulate healing frequencies in the physical, mental and emotional bodies, and even in the earth itself. Researchers working with sound have shown it can shape matter and create form. Adding devotion, feeling, visualization and heart to your emanations of sound creates Heartsound and multiplies your work untold times. And remember when this is done in groups, the work is squared by the number of people there.

4. The Power of THE VIOLET RAY

All energy we have ever used is marked with our personal frequency signature and always returns to us at some time. Energy that was wisely and correctly used adds to our attainment and energy account. Energy that was misused in any way is returned to us for purification. The use of this "joy flame" through visualization, prayer and mantra makes light work of the

201

otherwise difficult and painful process of transmuting the negative karma being returned to us.

5. The Power of CRYSTALS

The atomic lattice structure of crystals regulates the flow of electromagnetic energies passing through them. That's why silicon chips are used in computers and quartz crystals can be found in clocks, radios and microphones. Some types of crystals transduce electromagnetic energy into mechanical energy and vice versa. Sound energy can be converted to electrical impulses and back to sound again. Humans are electromagnetic beings and can therefore interact with crystals. Some crystals have properties that can cleanse our energies, while others can amplify them. They can transduce the sound energy of our toning and mantras into electromagnetic energy and transfer it through the crystal kingdom via resonance.

6. The Power of VISUALIZATION

The subconscious mind is our servant and can be programmed with vivid, detailed pictures. It's important to keep our mental images positive as much as possible because there's no such thing as an idle thought. Visualization for manifestation also requires consistency in the images. If we keep changing them it's like constantly changing the mold while the jello is trying to set.

7. The Power of FEELINGS

Feelings are the language of the universe; it responds to our feelings more than to our thoughts. Thought is used to generate feeling which can be encoded on sound to produce Heartsound. Feelings are magnets that can attract positive or negative circumstances depending on the nature of the feeling. Gratitude, joy and love are the most powerful positive energy attractors.

8. The Power of THETA

The slow theta brainwaves can enable a direct connection to the subconscious. In the theta state we can also go directly to the Source of all (if we can stay awake in this state). Either way it's a most fertile space for planting the seeds of commands or affirmations.

9. The Power of COMPASSION

Compassion is the practical application of love in daily living. Love is the currency of the universe; it's what we use to build a cosmic bank account of positive energy that we can draw on in the future. If earth is a school designed to hone and increase our capacity for love and compassion, we're definitely in an accelerated curriculum!

10. The Power of THE QUANTUM FIELD

At the subatomic quantum level everything is composed of and connected by waves encoded with information. Because the universe is thought to be holographic in nature, every change we make in ourselves is immediately reflected throughout the hologram. Our ability to affect change is immensely greater than we ever suspected.

11. The Power of CONSTANCY

Repetition and daily application build the energy matrix of our intention. Mere occasional use of these prayers and mantras would be no more effective than an occasional day of dieting or an occasional day of bodybuilding exercise: better than nothing, but not likely to achieve our aim. Set goals like 33, 40 or more consecutive days for your chosen prayer or mantra discipline. It's okay to take a short break before beginning the cycle again. As your goals are achieved, create new ones. Even if you achieve all your personal goals, the needs of the earth are great.

12. The Power of KUAN YIN

And finally, remember that, as the divine essence of compassion, Kuan Yin dispenses mercy and intercession to people of all faiths. By using her mantras with devotion to the Divine, we can access and amplify this healing force of compassion in our lives and throughout the earth.

Bibliography & Recommended Reading

Access the Power of Your Higher Self: Your Source of Inner Guidance and Spiritual Transformation,
Elizabeth Clare Prophet, Summit University Press, Corwin Springs, MT, 1997

A Happy Pocket Full of Money: Your Quantum Leap into the Understanding, Having and Enjoying of Immense Wealth and Happiness,
David Cameron Gikandi, Xlibris, Bloomington, IN, 2008

Alchemy of The Heart: How to Give and Receive More Love,
Elizabeth Clare Prophet and Patricia Spadaro, Summit Univ. Press, Corwin Springs, MT, 2000

All for the Love of God: Life with Mark Prophet, a Modern-Day Mystic,
Alex Reichart, Excelsior Publications, Virginia Beach, VA, 2008

A New Earth: Awakening to Your Life's Purpose,
Eckhart Tolle, Plume (Penguin), New York, NY, 2005

Bodhisattva of Compassion: The Mystical Tradition of Kuan Yin,
John Blofeld, Shamballa Publications, Boston, MA, 1977

Born a Healer: I Was Born a Healer, You Were Born a Healer Too!,
Chunyi Lin, Spring Forest Publishing, Minnesota, MN, 2003

Children Who Remember Previous Lives: A Question of Reincarnation,
Ian Stevenson, University Press of Virginia, Charlottesville, VA, 1987

Consciousness Beyond Life: The Science of the Near-Death Experience,
Pim Van Lommel, MD, Harper Collins, New York, NY, 2010

Crystal Healing: The Therapeutic Application of Crystals and Stones,
Katrina Raphaell, Aurora Press, New York, NY, 1987

Cymatics, A Study of Wave Phenomena and Vibration
Hans Jenny, MACROmedia Publishing, Newmarket, NH, 2001

Electrons: The Building Blocks of the Universe,
  Werner Schroeder, AMTF Publ., Mount Shasta, CA, 2002

Essence of The Heart Sutra: The Dalai Lama's Heart of Wisdom Teachings,
  Dalai Lama, Wisdom Publications, Boston, MA, 2005

Fast Food Nation: The Dark Side of the All-American Meal,
  Eric Schlosser, Houghton Mifflin, Boston, MA, 2001

Frequency: The Power of Personal Vibration,
  Penny Peirce, Atria Books, New York, NY, 2009

God is Not Dead: What Quantum Physics Tells Us about Our Origins and How We Should Live,
  Amit Goswami, Ph.D., Hampton Roads, Charlottesville, VA, 2008

Healing Mantras: Using Sound Affirmations for Personal Power, Creativity and Healing,
  Thomas Ashley-Farrand, Ballantine Wellspring, New York, NY, 1999

Healing Our Planet, Healing Ourselves: The Power of Change Within to Change Our World,
  Dawson Church and Geralyn Gendreau, Elite Books, Santa Rosa, CA, 2004

Healing Mudras: Yoga for Your Hands,
  Sabrina Mesko, Ballantine Publishing, New York, NY, 2000

Healing Words: The Power of Prayer and the Practice of Medicine,
  Larry Dossey, M.D., Harper Paperbacks, New York, NY, 1993

Heal Yourself with Breath, Light, Sound & Water: Ancient Healing Secrets
  Denis Ouellette, Natural Life News, Livingston, MT, 59047

Honor Yourself: The Inner Art of Giving and Receiving,
  Patricia Spadaro, Three Wings Press, Bozeman, MT, 2009

Joy of No Sex: Handbook for Higher Pleasure,
  Swami Bhaktipada, Palace Publishing, Moundsville, WV, 1988

Kuan Yin: Accessing the Power of the Divine Feminine,
    Daniela Schenker, Sounds True, Boulder, CO, 2007

Kuan Yin's Crystal Rosary (4 CDs and booklet),
    Elizabeth Clare Prophet, Summit University Press, Corwin Springs, MT, 1988
    (at Amazon.com)

Living in the Heart: How to Enter Into the Sacred Space Within the Heart,
    Drunvalo Melchizedek, Light Technology Publishing, Flagstaff, AZ, 2003
    (Incl. meditation CD)

Mantra Meditation: Change Your Karma with the Power of Sacred Sound,
    Thomas Ashley-Farrand, Sounds True, Boulder, CO, 2004 (Includes CD)

Matrix Energetics: The Science and Art of Transformation,
    Richard Bartlett, D.C., N.D., Atria Books, New York, NY, 2007

Memories of God and Creation,
    Shakuntali Modi, MD, Hampton Roads, Charlottesville, VA, 2000

Memories of Mark: My Life with Mark Prophet,
    Annice Booth, Summit University Press, Corwin Springs, MT, 1999

Opening to Meditation: A Gentle, Guided Approach,
    Diana Lang, New World Library, Novato, CA, 2004 (Includes meditation
    CD)

Paths of Light and Darkness,
    Mark and Elizabeth Clare Prophet, Summit University Press, Corwin Springs,
    MT, 2005

*Physics of the Soul: The Quantum Book of Living, Dying, Reincarnation and
    Immortality,*
    Amit Goswami, Ph.D., Hampton Roads Publishing, Charlottesville, VA, 2001

Quantum Reality: Beyond the New Physics, an Excursion into Metaphysics,
    Nick Herbert, Ph.D., Doubleday, New York, NY, 1985

Remarkable Healings: A Psychiatrist Discovers Unsuspected Roots of Mental and Physical Illness,
Shakuntali Modi, MD, Hampton Roads, Charlottesville, VA, 1997

Saint Germain, Master Alchemist: Spiritual Teachings from an Ascended Master,
Elizabeth Clare Prophet, Summit University Press, Corwin Springs, MT, 2004

Saved by the Light: The True Story of a Man Who Died Twice and the Profound Revelations He Received,
Dannion Brinkley, Harper Paperbacks, New York, NY, 1994

Secrets of the Light: Lessons from Heaven,
Dannion Brinkley, Harper One, New York, NY, 2008

Serpent of Light: Beyond 2012—The Movement of the Earth's Kundalini and the Rise of the Female Light,
Drunvalo Melchizedek, Red Wheel/Weiser Books, San Francisco, CA, 2007

Sound Medicine: The Complete Guide to Healing with the Human Voice,
Wayne Perry, Career Press, Franklin Lakes, NJ, 2007 (Includes CD)

Stones of the New Consciousness: Healing, Awakening & Co-creating with Crystals, Minerals and Gems,
Robert Simmons, Heaven and Earth Publishing, East Montpelier, VT, 2009

The 7 Secrets of Sound Healing,
Jonathan Goldman, Hay House Inc, Carlsbad, CA, 2008 (Includes CD)

The Ancient Secret of the Flower of Life, Volumes 1 and 2,
Drunvalo Melchizedek, Light Technology Publ., Flagstaff, AZ, 2000

The Book of Stones: Who They Are & What They Teach,
Robert Simmons with Naisha Ahsian, Heaven and Earth Publishing, East Montpelier, VT, 2007

The Conscious Universe: The Scientific Truth of Psychic Phenomena,
Dean Radin, Ph.D., Harper Collins, NY, 1997

The Dharani Sutra,
Master Hsuan Hua, Buddhist Text Translation Society San Francisco, CA, 1976

The Divine Matrix: Bridging Time, Space, Miracles and Belief,
Gregg Braden, Hay House, Carlsbad, CA, 2007

The Face on Your Plate: The Truth About Food,
Jeffrey Moussaieff Masson, W. W. Norton, New York, NY, 2009

The Field: The Quest for the Secret Force of the Universe,
Lynne McTaggart, Harper Perennial, New York, NY, 2002

The God Theory: Universes, Zero-Point Fields and What's Behind It All,
Bernard Haisch, Red Wheel/Weisser, San Franciso, CA, 2006

The Healing Power of Mudras: The Yoga of the Hands,
Rajendar Menen, Pushtak Mahal, New Delhi, India, 2007

The Healing Power of Sound: Recovery from Life-Threatening Illness Using Sound, Voice and Music,
Mitchell L. Gaynor, MD, Shamballa Publications, Boston, MA, 1999

The Healing Power of the Human Voice: Mantras, Chants and Seed Sounds for Health and Harmony,
Joseph D'Angelo, Joseph, Healing Arts Press/Inner Traditions, Rochester, VT, 2000. (Incl. CD)

The HeartMath® Solution,
Doc Childre and Howard Martin, Harper Collins, San Francisco, CA, 1999

The Holographic Universe: A Remarkable New Theory of Reality,
Michael Talbot, Harper Perennial, New York, NY, 1992

The "I AM" Discourses, Vol. 3,
Godfre Ray King, Saint Germain Press, Shaumburg, IL, 1940

The Intelligent Heart: Transform Your Life with the Laws of Love,
David and Bruce McArthur, A.R.E. Press, Virginia Beach, VA, 1997

The Intention Experiment: Using Your Thoughts to Change Your Life and the World,
Lynne McTaggart, Free Press, New York, NY, 2007

The Kuan Yin Oracle: The Voice of the Goddess of Compassion,
Stephen Karcher, Time Warner Books, London, England, 2001

The Marketing of Evil: How Radicals, Elitists and Pseudo-Experts Sell Us Corruption Disguised as Freedom,
David Kupelian, WND Books, Nashville, TN, 2005

The Masters and Their Retreats,
Mark and Elizabeth Clare Prophet, Summit University Press, Corwin Springs, MT, 2003

The Miracles of Archangel Michael,
Doreen Virtue, Ph.D., Hay House, Carlsbad, CA, 2009

The One Command: Command Your Wealth, Imprint Your DNA for Lasting Success,
Asara Lovejoy, Wisdom House, Dallas, TX, 2007

The Path to Immortality,
Mark and Elizabeth Clare Prophet, Summit University Press, Corwin Springs, MT, 2006

The Power of I AM: Creating a New World of Enlightened Personal Interaction,
John Maxwell Taylor, Frog Ltd., Berkeley, CA, 2006

The Quantum Shift in the Global Brain: How the New Scientific Reality Can Change Us and Our World,
Ervin Laszlo, Inner Traditions, Rochester, VT, 2008

The Road Less Traveled: A New Psychology of Love, Traditional Values and Spiritual Growth,
M. Scott Peck, MD, Simon & Schuster, New York, NY, 1978

The Science of the Spoken Word,
Mark and Elizabeth Clare Prophet, Summit University Press, Corwin Springs, MT, 1991

The Secret Power of Music: The Transformation of Self and Society Through Musical Energy,
David Tame, Destiny Books, New York, NY, 1984

The Self Aware Universe: How Consciousness Creates the Material World,
Amit Goswami, Ph.D., Tarcher/Putnam, New York, NY, 1993

The Story of a Soul, The Autobiography of St Thérèse of Lisieux,
Saint Thérèse of Lisieux, Image Books, New York, NY, 1957

The World Is Sound—Nada Brahma: Music and the Landscape of Consciousness,
Joachim Ernst Berendt, Nada Brahma, Destiny Books, Rochester, VT, 1983

ThetaHealing: Go Up and Seek God, Go Up and Work with God,
Vianna Stibal, Rolling Thunder Publishing, Idaho Falls, ID, 2007

Transcending the Speed of Light: Consciousness, QuantumPhysics and the Fifth Dimension,
Marc Seifer, Ph.D., Inner Traditions, Rochester, VT, 2008

Transforming Depression: The HeartMath® Solution to Feeling Overwhelmed, Sad and Stressed,
Doc Childre and Deborah Rozman, Ph.D., New Harbinger Publications, Oakland, CA, 2007

Transforming Stress: The HeartMath® Solution for Relieving Worry, Fatigue and Tension,
Doc Childre and Deborah Rozman, Ph.D., New Harbinger Publications, Oakland, CA, 2005

Unveiled Mysteries,
    Godfre Ray King, Saint Germain Press, Shaumburg, IL, 1939

Violet Flame to Heal Body, Mind, and Soul,
    Elizabeth Clare Prophet, Summit University Press, Corwin Springs, MT, 1997

Water Sound Images: The Creative Music of the Universe,
    Alexander Lauterwasser, MACROmedia Publishing, Newmarket, NH, 2006

Wheel of Great Compassion: The Practice of the Prayer Wheel in Tibetan Buddhism,
    Lorne Ladner, Wisdom Publications, Somerville, MA, 2000

Internet Resources

www.anopendooroflove.org (Compendium of ascended-master teachings)

www.avatarsandmasters.com (Compendium of ascended-master teachings)

www.cymaticsource.com (Cymatics: insights into the invisible realms of sound)

www.eftuniverse.com (Emotional Freedom Techniques®)

www.globalcoherenceinitiative.com (Uniting people in heart-focused care and intention)

www.heartmath.com (Official site of the Institute of HeartMath®)

www.heavenandearthjewelry.com (A good source for stones and crystals)

www.humanresonance.org (Much info on planetary changes, pyramids, etc.)

www.josefinestark.com (This author's web site)

www.kuanyinsmiraclemantras.com (web page to purchase this book in pdf form)

www.morrnahsimeona.com (Morrnah Simeona: Ho'oponopono Hawaiian healing)

www.naturallifenews.com (Alternative, natural healing methods, books, seminars, magazine, etc.)

www.newwisdomuniversity.com (Rev. Dawn Covington, Ed.D.: ascended-master teachings)

www.prosveta.org (Publishers of the works of Master Omraam Mikhaël Aïvanhov, 1900–1986)

www.rockymountainbiofeedback.com (Christine Meiner: "Natural healing through self-regulation")

www.sacredmysteriesbookstore.com (Books, statues, local lectures in Livingston, Montana)

www.sanatkumara.info (Expanding the mission of lightbearers, Therese Emmanuel Grey)

www.sanskritmantra.com (Sanskrit mantras and spiritual power)

www.siddham.org (A non-profit Buddhist information network)

www.soundstrue.com (Audios, books, seminars, etc.)

www.spiritualawarenessfellowship.org (Worldwide community sharing the spiritual path)

www.stagesingingsecrets.com (Performing skills for singers by this author, Josefine Stark)

www.templeofsacredsound.com (Jonathan Goldman, pioneer of sacred-sound therapy)

www.thetahealing.com (Vianna Stibal, ThetaHealing founder)

www.tsl.org (The Summit Lighthouse: teachings of the ascended masters)

Kuan Yin's Crystal Rosary, 4 CDs and booklet, includes the recitation in Chinese of the Ten Vows, The 33 Manifestations, and English songs and decrees, available from The Summit Lighthouse bookstore at www.tsl.org

www.worldwideashram.org (Ascended-master teachings originating with Mark Prophet)

About the Authors

Josefine Stark has been a Kuan Yin buff for more than two decades and has studied many mystical and spiritual paths both East and West for over four decades. During that time she has also researched quantum science and how this validates esoteric knowledge. She is a minister with Spiritual Awareness Fellowship, and has given lectures and workshops on Kuan Yin, affirmations, forgiveness and compassion and the violet light. Josefine had monthly articles published on a variety of subjects for five years in the *Montana Pioneer* newspaper. She has also taught acting classes and created the DVD set, *Acting Skills for Singers*, to teach performing techniques for singers in musicals, opera, etc. She lives in Bozeman, Montana.

Christine Meiner is a long-time student of the Ascended Master Teachings and quantum physics, and a Kuan Yin devotee. She has a Masters degree in Psychology and is a minister with Spiritual Awareness Fellowship. Christine is also licensed HeartMath® coach and Certified Hospice Worker. Christine has given personal development lectures and workshops in Sweden, Australia, and the United States. She currently resides in Montana.

Boyd Badten has been a student of the Ascended Masters' wisdom teachings for decades and is currently Director of Operations for the Hearts Center® spiritual movement. He frequently speaks on various aspects of meditation and the contemplative arts during spiritual gatherings. While visiting Buddhist temples in Taiwan in 2005, Boyd experienced a series of profound inner visions that brought back the memory of a previous life in China in which he was completely devoted to Kuan Yin. Since then, he has found it very easy to spiritually connect with Kuan Yin and to learn her emanation practices. Boyd resides in Montana with his family.

Shanti Hee was featured on the *Women of the Rainbow* TV series for Public Community Television in Honolulu from 2001 to 2004. Formerly a registered nurse, she now teaches and gives workshops on healing and spirituality. Her particular emphasis is on sound healing and toning. A devotee of Kuan Yin, she is also a natural intuitive and shares her personal and spiritual revelations to awaken people into remembrance of the Eternal Spirit. She was born in Hong Kong, resided in Hawaii, and has returned to China.

CPSIA information can be obtained
at www.ICGtesting.com
Printed in the USA
BVHW011858031218
534674BV00008B/338/P